AF478281

# ONION CREEK PHILOSOPHY

"POINTS OF PRACTICAL WISDOM"

By

CHARLES B. HODGE, JR.

Published By
BIBLICAL RESEARCH PRESS
774 East North 15th Street
Abilene, Texas
79601

# ONION CREEK PHILOSOPHY

## By Charles B. Hodge, Jr.

Library of Congress Catalog Card No. 79-87865
International Standard Book Number 0-89112-054-8

ii

# PREFACE

Charles Hodge has provided us in this volume with some prize insights into life, its meaning and values. He was reared as a boy down on Onion Creek, near Byrd, Texas, and much of his mature philosophy has come from those early experiences and influences.

These one-page lessons are Biblically based, but they do not lend well to grouping, and therefore a Table of contents would not be of value. They lend well to "Coffee Table" reading, since one can read them one or more at a sitting, with full value.

The lessons derive from a Bible-oriented mind, and one which seeks the betterment of mankind in an unselfish way. Therefore, as they penetrate into the real significance of the point being made, they challenge us with a powerful uplift.

J. D. Thomas,
Editor

# "ROOTS"

*"I am the God of Abraham, and the God of Isaac, and the God of Jacob? God is not the God of the dead, but of the living." —Matthew 22:32*

The literary and the TV worlds of 1977 were captured by *Roots.* All of us need a sense of identity! The Christian is no exception. Cults, fads, idols choke in the dust of time. Man cannot be fed by mythology . . . Christianity is set in history; God came as a man and acted upon the stage of history. Christians have "roots" that no one else has! Christianity is not a mere idea; it is not a human invention . . . Christianity happened. This present "Now generation" cares little for the past and less for the future. To them, it is all "now." But because of our "roots" we can claim tomorrow today!

Jesus Christ came to be born, Luke says, at a set time and specific place. History is important. This history is to be taught to our children (Deuteronomy 6:6-9). Who is going to teach our children? No one, not even our own children, become Christians automatically. Jesus is the seed of David, the seed of Jesse, the seed of Abraham! We must not spend all our attention upon obstetrics and neglect pediatrics! Newborn babes must be nourished with milk, then meat!

There is "no such an animal" as dull doctrine! It is the neglect of true Bible preaching that produces dullness. Everyone should know Adam's leaves, Noah's ark, Jacob's ladder, Joseph's coat, Moses' rod, Solomon's temple, Pilate's wash basin, and Paul's thorn! The River Jordan, the Upper Room, the Garden of Gethsemane, the Damascus Road . . . these are our "roots." Do you know? have you any roots?

## "LEADERS—THE BUCK STOPS HERE"

This author does not believe in combining church and politics . . . but he does believe in knowing what is happening . . . and since both politics and church involve *PEOPLE*— what is observed in one often happens with the other. For. instance, several key political men in Fort Worth have resigned recently. Now if only one had—but like dominoes, nearly all the key men have resigned! This tells you something—the "city followers" are not leading . . . they are demoralizing and driving key men from office! This means they are meddling, nit-picking, politicking, and pushing petty factions! Of all things, leaders must not demoralize the troops. Of all the responsibilities of leaders a chief one is encouragement! Encouraged men serve better; demoralized men serve less, then quit!

In the church, Bible teachers, preachers, other key men cease work and then ultimately quit? True, some should have never been selected. But why have some great men who served with profound zeal now "rust in pews"? This question must be asked—and answered! Why are some frustrated, yea embittered, in Church work? The answer again is discouragement! They worked zealously only to be "cut down," criticized, nit-picked, and left without support or appreciation. Of all things true on earth our dedicated workers should be encouraged, backed, and protected.

It bothers me downtown—but it bothers me more at Church!

# "GROWING OLD GRACEFULLY"

I constantly advise the young to choose an aged person whom they wish to be like. There is nothing more beautiful than a sweet, lovable older person. There is nothing more discouraging than a miserable, bitter, old person. We often get carried away telling youth of their duties and responsibilities—but most of us allow age to do awful things to us. As we grow older we will become a *peach* or a *prune*—the choice is ours.

Many of us get *worse* when we should improve with age. As time flies by we should get sweeter, cuter, mellower, and wiser. But some will become more rigid, narrow, and critical. Youth can communicate with older people who have youthful qualities. This is not in outward dress, or in the older person making a fool out of himself trying to be young. Youth resent this. Real "youth" is an inner quality, not a surface appearance.

It is tragic to forget what it was to be young. Not to have incorporated a youthful attitude into one's total personality. Nothing is more beautiful than an aged person who is both childlike and wise, spirited yet patient, still willing to learn while able to teach.

Socrates began taking dancing lessons at 70. Most of us just take dying lessons.

## "MAKE TODAY COUNT"

"Make Today Count" is an organization for the benefit of terminal patients and their families! How noble! A man is given but a few months to live. This group aids him and his family to "milk these final days for all their blessings." Actually this terminal "curse" can become a "blessing." It may be that a terminal patient has a PLACE he wishes to visit or a THING he wishes to do. But most people in their final days will come to grips with *REALITY!* What *does* really matter? Not trinkets, gadgets, pretense, the "rat-race" . . . but family, nature, friends–*GOD!*

This new organization encourages terminal patients to "Make Today Count." Hours are precious and not to be wasted! Conformism to modernity is "out the window." A person literally finds his life and himself! These final days can be spiritually rich, productive, and happy!

We conclude, "Isn't this wonderful for terminal patients?" But aren't we all "terminal patients"? "It is appointed unto man once to die!" Another preacher and I once visited a terminal patient in a hospital. But this "terminal patient" is yet alive–while the other preacher has since died with a heart attack! "The old *must* die–the young *may* die." All of us should join this group, "Make Today Count." Jesus taught this in Matthew 6:33, 34! Paul taught it in Philippians 3:13-14!

Don't wait until you get *sick* to *Make Today Count!*

# "AUTHORITY"

*"For he taught them as one having authority, and not as the scribes."* Matthew 7:29

**AUTHORITY!!** What is this that some have and others do not? Why is it that some can whisper with authority while others cannot shout with authority? Why will you respect some and not others? What is it that gives one authority? Why won't persons listen and follow you? Why do you fear a "mother's look" more than a "father's belt"? What is this quality Jesus had?

**AUTHORITY!!** Our text does not say Jesus was given it —He had it! There is a difference. If you gave it to some they still wouldn't have it! Fear is realistic and can be coped with; awe is supernatural and cannot. Authority is a rare gift; it cannot be counterfeited by fraud or substituted by force. We must choose leaders who have authority.

**AUTHORITY!!**

    (1) One must know his subject—of what he speaks.
    (2) One must deserve to be heard. He has earned the right to speak. Jesus did not preach until *30*.
    (3) One must be sincere and believe what he says.
    (4) One must be (practice) what he teaches.
    (5) One must care! This so often demoralizes—the teacher doesn't care! Jesus cared!

**AUTHORITY!!**

## "THE GREAT AND THE SMALL"

I like Allen Isbell—others may not, but I do. He puts out an interesting church bulletin (there are really few of them), covering everything from soup to nuts. The other week he had an interesting observation about Gilbert Scott, a renowned English architect. It seems Mr. Scott had just finished two projects—a cathedral and a telephone booth. Quite a difference; yet in *BOTH* there was the unmistakable sign of genius. As Allen said, "When a man learns to make something special out of a telephone booth as well as out of a cathedral, he has learned something important about life."

Man does not usually fail with the large, but with the small! We mind our "P's and Q's" with the important, but neglect the common. Such an attitude ruins life because most of life is routine and common. Every day is the most important day of one's life. Every person we meet is the most important person on earth. If we are taking out the garbage, we should do it with a "flair." Put a song in your heart and a smile on your face. Life need not be routine, stale, and dull. When a telephone booth is a challenge, then life is exciting!

Mind your appearance; take pride in a wholesome self-respect. Be a friend to all. Do every job with artistic pride . . . then satisfaction will fill your life. Jesus said, "Giving a cup of cold water" would have its reward.

Thanks, Allen, for your telephone-booth story!

**"ON LOVING ENEMIES"**

*"But I say unto you, love your enemies, bless them that curse you, do good to them that hate you and persecute you."* Matthew 5:44

This great verse has been glamorized as sentimentality or rejected as impossible. Both concepts misunderstand what Jesus taught.

(1) "Loving enemies" does not mean "liking them." This would be a burden no man could bear. No man can be commanded "to like." Enemies are still enemies—they are not now "allies."

(2) Loving an enemy may make of him a "friend." But if not, man cannot live in hate. I must love my enemy for "my sake" as well as his.

(3) To love means to be "lovable." One must not re-act but act. One must be Christian, regardless of how others are.

(4) To love is be like God rather than the Devil. Keep reading Matthew 5. Persons must learn that that which binds us together is greater than that which divides us.

(5) Enemies must be respected as opponents in contests. Regardless of your feelings toward others they must be given the liberty to play the game according to the rules. Merit is not just in behaving correctly with those we like. Compete in life as we do in games.

## "TIME"

"What I need is more time!" *TIME?* But more time cannot be created. It cannot be bought nor borrowed. Time cannot be printed like money. Time not used is spent; time, unlike money, cannot be saved for a rainy day. Time cannot be "speeded-up" nor "slowed-down." Time cannot be delayed.

(1) *TIME IS A RESOURCE.* All persons are equal—we have 24 hours in each day. Enough time daily to do well; not too much time to overwhelm or defeat us. Time is foundational to all other resources. A millionaire without time is bankrupt. Time is the raw material for everything. Therefore, of all the earth's resources, time is the most valuable. To waste time is to destroy life. Time is what life is made of. The trait common to all alleged "successful" men—is the usage of time. Productivity is simply the most output from the input.

(2) *"HOW-TO" BOOKS FAIL.* The issue is *WHAT,* not *HOW.* It is not "how fast can one read" but "what" is one reading! "What" is one doing with what he is reading? The negative is "what" not to read. The same is true of time. It is not "how to use time" but "what are you doing with time?" What is first, primary, eternal? Time determines eternity. "Man can gain the whole world, waste his time, and by so doing, lose his soul." "Busyness" is not necessarily "business."

Paul said, "Redeem the time."

# "SCHOLARLY LEGALISM"

Someone recently opined that the biggest problem we have is "Scholarly Legalism." "Nit picking" over every technicality. Being expert in "straining out gnats and swallowing camels."

This author feels that "Scholarly Legalism" has long plagued the Church. The Jews crucified Christ with "Scholarly Legalism" . . . they erred, not knowing scriptures nor the power of God. They accused Jesus of blasphemy. Now the Jews had the law, the OT Bible . . . they had "gone all over it with fine-tooth comb." They read it and quoted it as they rejected Christ.

Nearly all our church splits have come from "Scholarly Legalism." Charts, arguments, debates are held to uphold "Scholarly Legalism." The participants are eminent Bible scholars—yet they miss major truth!

The Bible—the Sword—cannot be sharpened in a church house—it must be sharpened in the world against real sinners. The Sword in the church house reduces itself to theology and "Church Policy." The Sword in the world becomes practical. One decision made in a back room of a church house cannot apply to the world in general. Life, truth, is sometimes situational! Jesus applied the right truth, the right principle to the person involved. He was not trying to protect "Church Policies" but to save and help sinners. People cannot be made to fit "paper" . . . people are more important than "Church Rules." Learn what this means, "I will have mercy and not sacrifice."

## "ANDREW—PLAYING SECOND FIDDLE"

Your author is not a musician—but they say the hardest instrument to play is "Second Fiddle." Few men can play this difficult position in life. All wish to be first, the best. But few can be number 1! The world's work is done by people in "Second Place."

Andrew is the "Mickey Mouse" brother of Peter! All know about Peter! Who knows about Andrew? He never made the "First Team." He never preached a recorded sermon nor wrote an inspired book. The three times he is on stage in the Bible were of little part. But notice what Andrew did not do!

(1) He didn't resign. This is human inclination number 1! Because you preach for a small Church does not make you a small man! Because you do a small job does not make you a small man. Great men with their great ministries actually never know it! This is true greatness. Andrew was great! Man makes the position; the position does not make the man.

(2) He didn't join the loyal opposition. He didn't begin criticizing Jesus, the elite 3, the 12! Andrew didn't even pick on Judas!

Andrew was great in all rights, himself! He was the first man called by Jesus! He was selected and called! He did find his brother, Peter! He did bring others to Jesus. He did evaluate conditions correctly.

A successful man said there are *57* rules of success. Number 1—"Deliver the Goods." Number 2—forget the other *56!* Andrew delivered the goods!

# "FINANCIALLY SPEAKING"

Brethren have always had problems with money . . . in the past preachers could not preach on giving . . . money was beneath our dignity . . . there could be no collections taken in a gospel meeting . . . preachers wanted to preach without pay . . . etc. But money is necessary to life. It is neither good nor evil—neutral. The Bible has no problems with money. It freely talks about it without apology. Jesus said more about money than any one subject. "It is more blessed to give than receive."

(1) We need to put our local church in our *will.* I have! I believe in Christian colleges and benevolent homes . . . but I have an obligation to my local church which I don't have to institutions. Is Christ in your will? Why not will some money, a house, a business to the local church? Does your insurance policy make provisions for the local church? Think of the evangelism, benevolence, mission work that could be done! Very, very few of us do this . . . so that what we supposedly love the most goes begging at "will time." Is Christ in your will? You were in His!

(2) Will your children have a Christian education? They can so easily. Is your child pre-school? Buy him a church bond—a compound interest bond. $3,000.00 in 9% compound interest bonds will be worth $7,236.00 in 10 years, or $11,235.00 in 15 years! You can borrow, with good credit, to obtain the $3,000.00! You cannot buy a car for that! Let's quit kidding ourselves . . . our children are deprived of a Christian college education because we did not plan, but we bought cars, vacations, and other pleasures!

Wake up, brethren, to the *GOOD* that can be done with money—*YOUR MONEY!*

## AFRAID OF STRENGTHS

It is true men are afraid of their *vices*—temper, whiskey, overeating, smoking, etc.; it is equally true (usually never considered) men are afraid of their *talents!* The "one talent" man hid his. Many talented men reject promotions, reject jobs of responsibilities, reject leadership roles. Many who could be great church workers sit on the sidelines—they are afraid of their strengths! This is evident many ways in the church:

(1) We are afraid of men who *think!* We like a Bible class of familiar comments with no challenge nor disagreement. True some are disruptive in classes—but is thinking encouraged? Is a thinker usually put down or run off? Many men who can think are never heard in church!

(2) We are afraid of men with *money!* It is true money oft times rules! But is it not also true much money is unconsciously rejected? Many wealthy men give elsewhere! There is resentment and jealousy.

(3) We are afraid of men of *action!* Men who constantly press for decision, changes, and good works are dangerous! They are fought and crucified many times. They rock the boat!

(4) We are afraid of *youth!* Youth are allowed to do little in church. Yet Six Flags makes millions with energetic, talented youth. (So far as I know they haven't taken over the Six Flags management!)

(5) We are afraid of *BIG MEN!* Great men of character, vision, kindness, wisdom, and patience are "cut down" by little, petty men running the church their way. Why must we be afraid of our strengths? When little men cast long shadows it is nearly sunset."

## "WINSTON CHURCHILL—ARE YOU READY?"

Winston Churchill was an interesting fellow! Among other things he said, "To every man there comes in his lifetime that special moment when he is figuratively tapped on the shoulder and offered that chance to do a very special thing, unique to him and his talents. What a tragedy if that moment finds him unprepared or unqualified for that work."

Recently an excited member told of the new preacher they had hired. He was so carried away—expecting the moon! Some preachers are sold for more than they are worth—the church pays. This man has moved like checkers the past few years, leaving split churches in his wake. They did not check that out nor will they—because they are "carried away." They are already defending him before he arrives!

Other preachers bloomed, then withered! Brotherhood figures of yesterday are gone today! Why? They were not ready nor qualified when "tapped." The situation exposed them with their weakness. It is amazing how brethren will be taken by a novice without experience! No track record—no dedication—no sacrifice—yet their voice determines the church. You cannot tell brethren anything—then they wonder why it all collapsed.

So a Christian studies, observes, grows, works—*AND WAITS!* Christ waited 30 years! Moses waited 80 years! Peter so often got ahead of himself! It is sad when the advice given is ahead of wisdom. When tapped—will we be ready?

## "READING"

"I just don't have time to read!" Have you heard this statement? Have you made it? Do you read? If so, what do you read? You cannot get class members to read the Bible for class studies! "I don't buy books." Have you heard or made that statement? "I don't even have time to read the Bible so why buy or read other books?" Have you heard or made that one? That is a cop-out! People who read the Bible read other books!

So publishers must be going bankrupt! It must be a terrible business without a future! Yet *MILLIONS—MILLIONS* of books are printed daily! *MILLIONS!* Every other page in the world is Communistic! Since 1917 Communism has taken one half of the world with the printed page! God put His revelation in a *Bible!* Never underestimate the power of the printed page! You read!!! Magazines, papers, hobbies, movies, sensational! You read!!! The problem is what you read!

Our reading declares we do not put first things first! We read the trivia, the second-place, to the dire neglect of the wise! We miss the great books to litter our minds with trash! *READ! READ!* But do not neglect the great books! The wisdom of *BOTH* heaven and earth can be in your hands!

A disappointed man was leaving a great art museum. He remarked, "Not a thing in here is worth seeing." The attendant answered, "These objects of art are no longer on trial—the spectators are!" *READ THE BEST!*

# "A PREACHER'S DEATH"

A local sectarian preacher died last Sunday morning while jogging. He was to have filled his regular pulpit; the parishioners did not know of his death until they arrived at church. This placed them in a state of shock! There are some observations from this:

(1) Death comes to one and all—and swiftly! Even a clergyman . . . on Sunday . . . prior to preaching. David said, "There is but one step between me and the grave." Death is certain—it is nigh, not distant! None will escape death!

(2) This "shock of reality" is not the foundation for conversion. True, some may think more soberly . . . but a "change" built upon fear may "make some want to stay out of hell, but not get them into heaven." Man must be converted at his strength—not his weakness. No emotional trauma will last. This preacher got more people to "his funeral" than he could get to "God's worship."

(3) Life and death are uncertain. This preacher and I happened to visit a mutual friend at a hospital in weeks past. The mutual friend has a terminal illness—he has been given one year to live at the most . . . but the preacher died before the patient!

The Bible does not teach "get ready," but "be ready." The Bible teaches all to "live" that they might "die." The Bible word is "watch." Are you ready?

# "OUR PRECIOUS CHILDREN"

*"Suffer the little children to come unto me, and forbid
them not, for of such is the kingdom of God"* Mark
10:14).

We love our children; we want to save our children; we
fret and worry about them . . . yet come high school gradu-
ation, a high percentage (over 50%) drop away from the
church! Why? This must be asked and answered. Jesus was
careful about children—He left favorable impressions.

The church has really never shared this importance of
children. We hire youth ministers and have youth rallies, but
our services and programs do not consider them. All a 5 year
old can see in worship when standing are knees and songbook
racks. His feet cannot touch the floor when seated. The
preacher talks in Hebrew and Greek. He is slapped when restless. Preachers give little thought to children in their sermons.
Most remember their early images of God as a punisher rather
than a rewarder.

Solomon said, "Train up a child in the way he should
go" (Proverbs 22:6). This is a beautiful farming symbol! A
mother cow helps her newborn calf by licking the calf's lips
with milk, creating a taste for milk. Parents should give
children a profound taste for God and the church. This must
be augmented by church worship and programs that "leave a
good taste in their mouths."

We will never save the world until we are able to save our
children.

# "GRANDPA HODGE HERE"

By now the whole world knows (or should) that I have a grandson! *MARVELOUS!* Nothing on earth like it! God has such a beautiful way of re-enforcing His great truths:

(1) *LIFE.* The *POWER* of God made Adam from dust; no less *POWER* delivers babies from wombs. *LIFE–LIFE–LIFE!* Only God produces *LIFE!* Man is humbled at both the crib and the cemetery. There is a Sovereign God in whom we live, move, and have our very being! There is a God to whom we account! Babies remind us about LIFE/GOD/JUDG-MENT!

(2) *UNCONDITIONAL LOVE.* Man seems to think that *GRACE, UNCONDITIONAL LOVE, ACCEPTANCE* are beyond man's comprehension! But of the 10-30 babies in the nursery Hodge saw only one! He has yet to handle this baby! But he will already die for this little intruder! He loves this child profoundly–*UNCONDITIONALLY!* Size, color, IQ, have nothing to do with it! That child would have been loved however he came! This child cannot earn, buy, negotiate for Grandpa's love! It is there; regardless as to what the future holds–this love will abide! No one, nothing can cause my committed love for him to cease!

This explains God's love toward me! It has nothing to do with size, color, or IQ! God's love cannot be bought, earned, nor negotiated. Nothing can hinder God's love. We must know this and revel in this. This is our motivation for goodness and obedience–because God loves us! God reaffirmed this so beautifully to Ole Hodge with Gregory Bryan! He will never forget it.

# "WHAT KIND OF TEACHER ARE YOU?"

Women are to be "teachers of good things" (Titus 2:3). Truth is to be trusted to faithful men that they might teach (2 Timothy 2:2). There is a special judgment (responsibility) for teachers (James 3:1). *TEACHERS!* What memories—good and bad—this word projects! Someone has said there are three kinds of teachers.

(1) *THOSE WHO ARE NEVER REMEMBERED!* For a year in Bible class they were your teacher . . . but there is no lasting impression. Their preparation was meagre, their presentation boring, they never knew your name, they never called nor visited . . . they just were "teachers" because someone put them in a class! What are your goals for the class? for each students? Do you care? Do you really prepare and inform? Do you really love your class? your students? Any class can be exciting without exceptional talent—benign neglect ruins classes and teachers!

(2) *THOSE WHO ARE NEVER FORGIVEN!* A teacher should not automatically make students hostile! Some think all students are "out to get them." They react—they teach on the defensive! They do not allow questions—they "cram" answers down throats without allowing reply. Many people today stay away from churches because of tyrannical teachers! You can *command* respect but not *demand* it!

(3) *THOSE WHO ARE NEVER FORGOTTEN!* Thank God for these precious people! These that loved us and taught us! Christianity is both *taught* and *caught!* Exciting classes because the teacher cared. Your editor was blessed with some great teachers. Every year he writes a letter to one who taught and made him who he is! These teachers teach—they must teach—it must come out! Which kind of teacher are you?

# "ON LEARNING TO LOVE"

I ordinarily pay little attention to Joe Schubert—his wife surely doesn't—but an article of his in a recent *Power For Today* really makes sense. Now Joe didn't think it up—he got it from June Callwood's, *Love, Hate, Fear, Anger, and the Other Emotions.* She observes, "Love takes thirty years to learn. Love is the only emotion that isn't natural, the only one that has to be learned, and the only one that matters."

The Bible word for this love is "agape." It is in the will—not the glands. It is not poetic romance. The Bible commands mates to love each other—yea their children. Brethren are to love each other, yea even their enemies. *LOVE!* It takes time, effort, and experience.

We have not actually taught our children to love. We find it difficult to *love* those we do not *like*. We don't work at it. Until of late fellowship halls have been considered suspect—a luxury of softness. Our crying need is to "love the brother-hood." Some of us like our local church—but the brother-hood??

The lady said it takes 30 years! Let's try it!

## "IF YOU CANNOT AFFORD IT YOURSELF—
## YOU CANNOT AFFORD SOMEONE
## TO GIVE IT TO YOU"

*MONEY!* You cannot live "with it" or "without it." *MONEY!* People have always searched for the "pot of gold at the end of a rainbow" . . . they search for gold, instant wealth, get-rich-quick schemes, something for nothing. Papers headline the lotteries, inheritances, quick success. All watch TV programs hypnotized—with jealousy. A black man found an armored car money bag with millions! He turned it in— the general public harrassed him out of their community.

But men with instant money have tremendous problems! Divorce, alcoholism, suicides follow men with instant wealth. Daddy always said, "If you cannot afford it yourself—you cannot afford someone else to give it to you." It makes sense!

*WHY?* Because instant money demands a change in life-style! This is the invisible problem with instant success or instant wealth! Men can get "too much too soon." Any trinket that alters your life style involves problems. Would it drastically change your life? Can you handle it? Is it worth it? Very few can handle a change in life style.

"If you cannot afford it yourself—don't accept it from someone else—don't covet it."

# "DISCIPLES ANONYMOUS"

One of my hobbies is collecting epitaphs on tombstones. In old cemeteries, especially, one sees the contradiction, "Gone but not forgotten." Men have spent fortunes erecting marble monuments at the graves of loved ones. David said, "I am forgotten, as a dead man" (Psalms 31:12). *MAN WANTS TO BE REMEMBERED!* It humiliates us not to be remembered by a past acquaintance! It seriously wounds our pride!

*FACE IT!* Most of us will go into eternity anonymously —"Gone *and* forgotten." Newspapers every day report "an unidentified" someone did something . . . but the point is— it was done! Most things will be done by "unidentified people." Very few will be remembered even 10 years hence.

Jesus sent out the seventy—we do not know their names. But man has to "come up with a name." The "Three wise men" have been named—although the Bible does not even say there were three! The "Rich Young Ruler" has been identified by some scholars as John Mark—actually without any foundation. The thieves crucified with Christ have also been given names without any scripture or reason. Whose wedding feast did Jesus attend in John 2? Who is the famous preacher in 2 Corinthians 8:18-19? Man wishes to name that which is important; he wishes to be named to be important!

So, even while alive, your author is often faced with "Hodge Who?" Even the Yankees forgot Joe Dimaggio. Only *ONE* person is to be remembered—*JESUS!* He gave to the church the Lord's Supper . . . this *REMEMBERS* Him until He comes!

# SURRENDER BEFORE COMMITMENT

We all have good intentions; we have all been restored at one time or another. We start with flaming enthusiasm only to cool down to apathy. *WHY?* Why bring in another charismatic preacher to give us the "guilts"? *WHY?* Why do "once active" members quit? Why cannot we finish what we begin? We preach "Commitment, commitment, commitment" yet this does not characterize us. *WHY?*

Because "surrender" precedes commitment! We must die to self (self denial). Even Jesus taught denial before cross bearing. Jesus is not to be accepted only as our "Personal Savior"? He is also to be accepted as our "Personal Lord!" We have not taught the Lordship of Christ. To confess Christ as Lord is to confess His life (character) and its claims upon ours! We should surrender before we commit.

This is the problem in difficult marriages! The couple "committed" without surrender to each other! This is the problem with preachers, and church workers who start, then quit. They committed themselves to the project without personal surrender!

So in life we "start and stop," "stop and go," "renew then quit," "off-again/on-again." Commitment is necessary . . . *YES!* But "commitment without surrender fails." Let's teach *SURRENDER!*

# "A LEFT-HANDED COMPLIMENT"

Our daughter Sherri came home for the holidays telling about fellow students who knew or had heard about me. That's a sort of "right-handed" compliment. But then she said they invariably asked, "Is your Dad liberal or conservative?" She asked me how to answer. I told her, "Tell them I am a Christian."

Herein is the compliment: Sherri didn't know! A man is who he is "at home!" I hadn't been extreme at home. My coterie of close friends are not extreme. There is no party spirit at the Hodge house! This is the compliment. I am neither liberal nor conservative . . . just Christian.

But the fact of the question bothers me. We who preach "only a Christian and a Christian only" are getting into the "label business." That's wrong! You are not to be a "liberal Christian" or a "conservative Christian." The very words of our speech are not in the Bible. On any given day I am liberal *and* conservative. Liberal or conservative to what? I am liberal compared with some and conservative with others. This is human branding.

So liberals get together and laugh about conservatives; and conservatives laugh at liberals. There is more allegiance to "party spirit" than to Christ. Liberals get more liberal and conservatives get more conservative. Pressure is exerted to line up members, churches, papers, and schools.

How pathetic! This was the crime at Corinth—"members of Paul, Apollos, Peter!" Paul "climbed the wall" denouncing this petty carnality. A great compliment! I'm so glad my own daughter hadn't branded me liberal or conservative!

## "EVERYBODY ANSWERS TO SOMEBODY"

Guyana, the "Moonies," now at Sherman/Denison—Why do people choose to blindly follow dictators??? We must always remember we are in the "People" business. "People" do not fit on "paper." Our mistakes and shocks are people mistakes.

"Everyone answers to someone." This is truth incarnate! Adam and Eve rebelled against this truth! Atheism is the ultimate in denial! Sin is simply saying, "I will not answer to anyone or anything." Teens hate and rebel against this fundamental. The feminist movement is a present application. Hedonism, liberalism—all are denials! Preachers answer to elders; elders answer to the congregation that selected them. Elders can even be called down by preachers (1 Timothy 5:20). Jesus is the only person who was safe without accountability! Yet He rejected the very notion! He commanded John to baptize Him! He was not content with His own judgment—He always sought out the will of God! No one is above the law! We must all give account!

The converse that "People Savvy" is equally true. People resign from personal responsibility! They follow the world (Romans 12:1, 2), peer pressure . . . worse still—cults like in Guyana. Their lives are completely turned over to a demon! It is amazing the power some have over others!

"Everyone answers to someone." The issue is "to whom!" To whom do you answer? Man is safe only under the will of God. Find it.

## "JOY"

Christianity is joy! Too many make Christianity weary and routine—they do the impossible—they make Christianity dull! The kingdom is joy (Romans 14); the fruit of the Spirit is joy (Galatians 5); Paul tells us to rejoice (1 Thessalonians 5).

In Greek *charis* is grace; *chara* is joy! They are twins. The "grace of God" brings "joy to man." One of the words for forgiveness is *charizomai*. To be forgiven is the satisfaction of profound joy. The Gospel is "Good News" not "Bad News." There is enough gloom in the world without making the Gospel an additional burden! There are problems, hurts, failures in life—hell is eternal—but Christ is the answer! So be happy!

But look at worship! We clothe ourselves uncomfortably and sit in hard pews and get into an unfavorable attitude, then complain that our worship is not what it ought to be! Fellowship and joy of the saints produce worship! Worship is joy—not just a duty!

We did not get this attitude from Jesus! He was at banquets in Galilee; He was sought out by all kinds of people. Above all—He attracted little children! Little children in a sense are great "character judges." They do not gather around grouches! Adults may, out of politeness—but not children!

**JOY!!**

# MAN IN THE IMAGE OF GOD

We continue our study of man made "like" God. We have already learned that man is not like God physically and in many ways is "unlike" God. This should eliminate false concepts of heaven. Man in heaven will still be man—not God! Man will be "like angels" in heaven yet not an angel (Matthew 22:29-30)! Man will neither be "all-knowing" nor "all-powerful" in heaven. He will still not be "God," but a worshipper, a creature, of God.

Again, man fallen in sin is still "in the image of God." "Therewith bless we God even the Father; and therewith curse we men, who are made after the likeness of God" (James 3:9). Man in sin has not lost "this image."

How, then is man like God? (1) Man is rational. Birds and animals have instincts. Birds fly as always and salmon return, as always. Man is rational—he can learn, progress, and grow. Man can change. A dog is a dog forever; man can become less than a man. This is the calamity of man's sin, in Genesis 3. Man abdicated his reasoning before a serpent. Consequently the truth makes man free (John 8:32). Man is transformed and renewed in his mind (Romans 12:1, 2).

(2) Man is moral. He can be good or bad. He can discern between good and evil. Man has conscience. This inspires him to honesty and condemns transgression. Man is "like" God in morality.

(3) Man can choose. Being able to know, man must choose. He is free to choose—either heaven or hell. Man is neither animal nor robot—he is man, made in the image of God.

What a great privilege and responsibility!

## "ENCOURAGEMENT"

Someone went to a "Garage Sale in Hell" . . . Satan was selling out . . . he had many interesting things—deceit, slander, meanness. But the highest price was on something that could not be recognized—it was the tool "discouragement." Satan's greatest tool is discouragement! All he has to do to ruin is to discourage.

The greatest commodity needed in the church today is "encouragement." We have too many who know "what's wrong" rather than "what's right." Negativism, pessimism, cynicism are the order of the day. Good works are shouted down; Church workers get demoralized. Leaders forget or neglect the one great tool—encouragement.

Jesus was one who encouraged—He saw potential, he presented goals, and he expected. Peter became rock and Matthew preached. Jesus encouraged children, the ill, sinners, widows, and disciples. He remained confident though others quit!

Barnabas is called "The Encourager." He found Saul in Tarsus when he had been forgotten! He rescued John Mark when he had been rejected! He was always giving to and promoting someone else.

Paul was encouraging. His letters always began and ended with a positive note! He wrote to his "preacher boys" with encouraging words!

Kind notes, complimentary remarks, thoughtful actions keep Hodge preaching! Loveable people are sought out on dark days. They encourage and enrich. It does not take talent to encourage—only a lovely Christianity! Practice it!

# "TOO CONSERVATIVE!"

*"He that observeth the wind shall not sow; and he that regardeth the clouds shall not reap."* Ecclesiastes 11:4

More and more people are saying, "It is wiser to be conservative," "he is a good conservative." Now in certain areas this is wise, but prudence can also destroy! The church perhaps is hurt more from doing nothing than in being reckless! Lives are dull and dead because risk is entirely removed. Many are dead while they live.

In other words some may fail in too much zeal, but they also may fail in too much prudence! Some may fail in over-recklessness but most in over-prudence. Some cannot eat because of ecology! Nader's Raiders have us Americans afraid to breathe! Environmentalists will starve to death! Jesus said, "Let the dead bury the dead." He wanted the would-be volunteer to "launch out."

Some of us cannot see the work for the problems. Some cannot see the good for the bad. Some know "what's wrong" but not "what's right." The one-talent man buried his talent in prudence. We talk about the peril of genius—but Jesus damned mediocrity.

It is easy to see the fanaticism of a fool—but can we also see the foolishness of caution? It is better to try and to fail, then to do nothing and criticize.

# "TO LOVE AND TO BE"

Jesus was practical and simple. He reduced happy living to two obvious things, "loving" and "being." But the keys to success are equally the keys to failure. Men make or break themselves with these two fundamentals.

*TO LOVE.* We want love but often times do not give it. Daily, melancholy people cry, "No one loves me." Lonely, bitter, frustrated people. They have "painted themselves into a corner." What can you do or what do you do with such people? Jesus loved! Everyone, everywhere, every time. But this was not in general! It was not idealistic. He loved self, family, neighbors, country, yea enemies. He dared love—and He changed the world. The Christian's badge is to love as He loved (John 13:34, 35). Only self-less people who love, are happy.

*TO BE.* Others cry in futility, "No one needs nor wants me." To feel oneself worthless is lamentable! We are success mad—not character interested. The Bible says, "be perfect," "be steadfast," "be strong," "be holy." Jesus gave the Beatitudes (Matthew 5). Recently during a shoe shine, a man commented about his son in college. He criticized the cost, but he added, "It will help him make money." What a pitiful reason to gain an education—not to be a more useful person but a richer man. The man then added, "My son changed his major to _______, because there's more money in it."

*TO LOVE AND TO BE.*

# OUR AMAZING UNIVERSE

Lon Woodrum had a fascinating article recently in *Christianity Today* titled, "Beyond the Quasars." It was an article to build faith. Since I am not scientific, such articles enthrall and renew. In our universe outposts there are quasars, pulsars, supernovas, galactic clusters, neutron stars, and black holes. Some scientists think we are at "the edge of the universe."

But the "terms" for celestial bodies! A quasar is capable of producing more energy than a *BILLION SUNS!* A pulsar (residue of a burned out star) weighs a *BILLION TONS* per one cubic inch! *STAGGERING!*

A quasar is so distant that what we see burned 10 million light-years ago! "Light-years" are bounced around on our tongues without realization as to immensity. Say "earth" and while saying it light has traveled around our planet several times! One light-year is *six trillion miles!* Now multiply that by billions! The size, energy, and beauty of our universe is mind-staggering.

Yes, it is big, but not nearly as big as the *GOD* who made it! Out there—there is more than *SOMETHING*—there is *SOMEONE!* This world cannot be an unexplained accident! Why should we doubt the ability of a God who makes quasars! God is on our side; He is in control; He knows . . . and best of all . . . He will keep His word.

## "HANDLING RISKS"

Life to be exciting and successful involves *"DARE."* As people and congregations age, they become more cautious and conservative. They lose the power of the "risk"—"nothing ventured nothing gained." What have you dared, risked lately? There are four kinds of "risks" in life:

(1) *RISKS ONE MUST ACCEPT.* They involve daily living. To get to the office you face the risk of being run over by a car. You can fail at home or on the job or at school. You cannot chain yourself in the back room and withdraw from life. Life involves rejection, failure, hurt, illness, and ultimately death. These must be accepted.

(2) *RISKS ONE CAN AFFORD TO TAKE.* If you are rich you can afford to risk a few dollars in a venture. We must take risks as our children grow and cut apron strings.

(3) *RISKS ONE CANNOT AFFORD TO TAKE.* Teenagers—you cannot afford the risks of drugs, petting, drinking, games of "chicken," going against what your parents are, going against what the church is and expects. Too many are paying too high a price for the "Far Country."

(4) *RISKS ONE CANNOT AFFORD NOT TO TAKE.* There are "risks" that must be taken! Be baptized because you can "hold out." Be restored because you can be forgiven and used by God. Launch out because God blesses men of faith. Abraham, Moses, David, Paul risked all they had and counted it as dung! Some of you are miserable—you haven't dared, risked, ventured, walked by faith. Make the "leap of faith."

# "SELF MANAGEMENT"

In our incredibly complex and fast-moving world all of us need to examine our goals, our motivations, our directions. What is truly important? All of us declare what has priority, then overrule that priority with trivia! We all know our goals but we waste our lives upon minor matters!

Philosophy has said, "Know thyself," "To thine own self be true," "Physician, heal thyself." But most of us refuse to stop, examine, and evaluate. It usually takes a crisis, a tragedy, or a blunt confrontation with reality to make us honestly evaluate. *STOP! THINK! WHAT IS IMPORTANT?*

What are your real goals? How do they incorporate themselves into your values? Are they for real—or for show? At 40-50 many are bitter, wondering where time and opportunity have gone. Are you giving 90% of your time and resources to real goals? What percentage? Most of us defer thinking with, "There will be time tomorrow."

Can you accept defeat? loss? One mark of a great man is his capacity to manage disappointment and loss. Most of us say *people* are more important than *things,* but do we find time for *people?*

Do we care? Love—or the capacity to care—is the only antidote to hate we know. What is the role of love in your life? Can we care? Do we have the capacity to care? Do we invest ourselves in others? get involved with others? listen to others? Do we care about others? How well do I love (like) myself? Relationships mirror self. I am to love my neighbor as myself. Am I fulfilling myself?

## "MAGNANIMITY"

Next to the Bible and the daily paper, folks should read the *Readers' Digest!* Concise, funny, practical, and stimulating. Something for everyone. The May issue had an outstanding article, "The Noblest of Human Graces." An audience was asked to express their most respectable personality trait—the answers were varied—humility, forgiveness, patience, etc. But *NOT ONE* mentioned the great and rare MAGNANIMITY!

It means, "High souled, rising above pettiness or meanness; generosity in overlooking injury or insult."

Who was Christ—*THE* man of magnanimity! The *BIGGEST, BESTEST* MAN who ever lived! Christ's life is summed in one word—magnanimity. "Love your enemies, bless them that curse you, pray for them who abuse you." "Turn the left cheek, go the second mile." "Forgive them, they know not what they do." Paul added, "overcome evil with good" (Romans 12). History's great men were magnanimous men. Abraham Lincoln appointed his worst enemy Secretary of War. Booker T. Washington said, "I will permit no man to narrow and degrade my soul by making me hate him." Robert E. Lee walked to the church altar when a black man came forward!

It is easier to re-act, to fight back, to be little! What really could the church be if all were magnanimous!

> He drew a circle that shut me out
> Heretic, rebel, a thing to flout.
> But love and I had the wit to win,
> We drew a circle that took him in.

# "STAYING IN LOVE"

I don't know why—doubt if anyone does—where the idea or statement "falling in love" originated! Whoever or wher-ever—it is wrong—and silly if it is right! "Falling" means accidental, downward, failure. So one would not wish to "fall in love" even if it were correct! But authors, song writers, romanticists have capitalized and sold it! "Falling in Love is Wonderful," the songs say. So all of us wish to "fall in love." Some even try.

But most are not interested in "staying in love." But this is the issue! Anyone can "fall in love" . . . few "stay in love." But love endures! Love never fails! Love is permanent. There has never been, so far as I know, a novel, essay, or song glamorizing "staying in love." Staying in love is not spectac-ular; it demands hard work, sacrifice, and endurance. It can be "plain Jane" much of the time. Love grows as it stays.

(1) We must "stay in love" in marriage. Some people who "fell in love" did not "stay in love." It must be "worked at." The price may be high.

(2) We must "stay in love" at church. Few remain zealous over a 10 year span. The issue is not "falling in love" with a project, but "staying in love."

(3) Preachers and local churches must "stay in love." This would insure tenure. Let's all "stay in love."

# "UNREQUITED LOVE"

*"And I will very gladly spend and be spent for you; though the more abundantly I love you, the less I am loved."* 2 Corinthians 12:15

Unrequited love—the tragic truth of life! How difficult a lesson to learn, to accept, to overcome! So many have felt its hurt—God is the Chief Sufferer of the universe. He loves so much and receives so little!

All of you know such situations . . . a mate loves dearly, only to be betrayed and deserted. Loving parents sacrifice, only to have ungrateful children. Men build a school, a town, a club, only to have it "turn upon them."

Such a tragedy overtook the Apostle Paul! He evangelized Corinth (Acts 18), remaining 18 months with a church composed of the vilest sinners (1 Corinthians 6). He built tents and robbed other congregations (2 Corinthians 11) to preach for them! They cared less! They turned to other hirelings, accusing Paul of being a hireling, a poor speaker, a poor worker, and so on! Yet Paul was willing to "spend and be spent."

Why is it that dedicated persons are abused while religious shysters are rewarded? Why is it faithful preachers are stoned while charlatans are followed? It is ironic that those most dedicated to "doing right" are blinded by the flattery of church hirelings! It never ceases to amaze me. Yet the innocent suffer! Jesus said, "Woe unto you, scribes and Pharisees, hypocrites! for ye devour widows' houses, and for a pretence make long prayer; therefore ye shall receive the greater damnation" (Matthew 23:14).

# CHURCH AUDIENCES

Several hundred members and friends gather to worship . . . one man preaches . . . the others listen. The Bible is interested in hearers—"how you hear," "what you hear." There is a commensurate obligation upon the hearer as well as the speaker. Audiences can be divided into at least four distinct kinds:

(1) *SPONGES.* Sponges "soak up" everything they touch. These hearers listen, read, accumulate notes and facts. They become "walking encyclopedias." They are curious and technical enjoying talk sessions. Alas, they know "everything and nothing." They do not change, grow, apply. They "soak up" like sponges.

(2) *FUNNELS.* These are hearers wherein truth "comes in one ear and goes out the other." They "tune out" the unwanted and demanding. People become angered when told the things they know yet do not wish to know! They become funnels and lose their chance to learn.

(3) *STRAINERS.* There are hearers so technical and nit-picking they strain out the good and remember the bad. One statement, one word, one something-or-another riles them. All they remember is that one bad thing.

(4) *SIFTERS.* There are hearers that are explorers, hunters, seekers. They "wade through" the chaff to find "pearls of great price." They seek for wisdom, practical applications for truths presented. They make speaking worthwhile. What part of the audience are you?

## "NUMBER 1 TRIES HARDER"

AVIS long has advertised—"When you're number 2—you have to try harder." If you are like me—you accepted this as truth without thought. I thought—it ain't true! For months I was number 1 on the Handball Challenge Ladder. All below can challenge—if they win they become number 1. This makes me number 2!

(1) No one brags about being number 2! If you are not number 1 you don't really care if you are number 2 or number 6. No one fights and claws to be number 2! You don't even challenge a man to get number 2!

(2) You try harder—you are number 1! You play harder —knowing number 1 is at stake. When tired, preoccupied, hurt—you could play just to play. But you pay a price to maintain number 1! If defeated it was still at your best effort! The other fellow just "outdid you."

(3) There is pride! You are number 1! There are expectations! This is not vanity—it is personal pride. You are representing number 1! You expect more from Madison—or Broadway! Why? Because of who they are. People and congregations must develop this personal expectation.

(4) You are more honest. It is disgusting to see petty tricks—yea cheating—used to get to be number 1! But if they cheated to get there they are still not there.

(5) You are more gracious. You must be magnanimous. You are at the top. There is an attitude and spirit appropriate.

The number 1 has to try harder!

## "IT WENT TO HIS HEAD"

There are many "Countryisms" that do not exactly tally! Why should success "go to a man's head"? If it went to his head (sense) he could handle it. Or could he? Paul did say in the Bible that "knowledge puffs up." So maybe pride does literally "go to the head."

There are some observations to make: (1) Homer Herring has a statement, "his knowledge exceeds his wisdom." Education, degrees, are neutral—they can neither make nor break! But it has "ruined some" in our definition. This is so tragic—so contradictory. But IQ and wisdom are two different things. Intelligent people can be stupid! Don't let it go to your head!

(2) Some have physical beauty or special abilities. Psychology says beautiful people make better grades, taller men get better jobs. There are all kinds of jokes about "dizzy blondes," suggesting that beauty and brains don't mix! Reggie Jackson can knock homeruns but he is a repulsive person. War heroes rarely live up to their herosim. Don't let it go to your head!

(3) Some acquire money, and it exceeds their character! Why should success change you? Your life style? Why should any have snobbery? Can you handle success? Money? Don't let it go to your head! John simply said, "May you prosper as your soul prospers." Don't let anything exceed your religion.

# "ZEALOTS"

Zealots make history exciting! There was a "Zealot" party in Judaism at the time of Christ . . . fanatical, extreme, bold, unbending. Right or wrong, they are exciting. On the handball court recently an opponent gave me a definition of a zealot, "Logically, down deep he knows he is wrong, but emotionally he sincerely thinks he is right." This is provocative . . . think about it!

A great illustration of this in sports was revealed this week! A relatively unknown sprinter ran 100 yards in 9 flat! The first and only time it was ever done! The world's fastest human! But expert track purists deny it! Yes—deny it! They say it wasn't done. The track was measured and was 100 yards; the wind was not violated; the sprint was video taped; 4 judges all timed it . . . there is no logical way to deny it!!! Why deny it? Well, it happened in Knoxville (no name in sports) . . . the sprinter is unknown . . . track purists didn't bother to attend. So in "track pride" they deny it!

There are certain things that are *wrong*, but the arguments why they are wrong are *equally wrong!* We know they are wrong, but for wrong reasons! This makes hypocrites of us all. So one can become *wrong* even when he is *right!* There are other things we make *wrong* when they are *right!* Down deep, we know we are wrong, but emotionally we defend ourselves with all our being. *ZEALOTS!*

# "PUT ON YOUR MITTENS"

Children always know in the wintertime what their mothers will say as they go out to play, "Put on your mittens." It is good advice for a cold day; it is also good advice for a cold soul:

*ADMIT* Christianity is reality; spirituality is reality. Jesus did not come in a fantasy. He became sin in a world of sin; He was tempted in all points. He ran the gamut of human emotions. God is integrity (light); nothing in Him is hid. We look and admit honestly in confession. "Put on your mittens."

*SUBMIT* The hallmark of Christianity is submission (Ephesians 5:21). All members submit to all members. No man may set himself above the duty of submitting his will and judgment to that of his fellows. The church (humanly speaking) belongs to the members. "Put on your mittens."

*COMMIT* This is the land of everything "instant." The experience of the Holy Spirit without discipline and time and maturity and price. Glory without sacrifice. Sex without marriage. People want all of the benefits without sharing the responsibility. "Put on your mittens."

*TRANSMIT* Genuine life must be shared; man was not made to be alone. Only with others can he find himself. Man shares his life, his knowledge, his soul. This is fellowship— sharing our lives with and for others.

"Put on your mittens."

## "DRINKING DRIVERS"

Jim Murray is a sportswriter—not a preacher. He is a social drinker—not a crusader. He writes for the *Los Angeles Times*. He recently devoted an entire column to drinking drivers.

His analogy—the great Indy 500! He suggests the average man would be "white with fear" if he had to drive in that august race. Then he said you would be safer there than driving on the Los Angeles freeway. In Los Angeles after midnight *one of five* drivers are drunk and *one of two* have been drinking! He said, ". . . over 50 per cent of highway fatalities are caused by alcohol in the tanks—and I don't mean the gas tanks."

"Any race driver, from Foyt to Jones, knows that the first-time driver is the most dangerous one at Indy. Well, so is the first time drinker."

He then tells of a test in California, "How Drinking Affects Your Driving." They used *two* professional drivers. After a sober run they each drank a half pint of vodka. They knocked over the rubber cones directing the course. They also found, via tests, that men drive faster under alcohol when the traffic is worse.

So, don't drink and drive!

Better yet—don't drink!

## "CURSING OUR BLESSINGS"

*"They have disregarded my sabbaths, so that I am profaned among them. Therefore, I have poured out my indignation upon them; I have consumed them with the fire of my wrath. "* Ezekiel 22:26,31

Ezekiel 22 is horrible—frightening—terrible! God is mad —real mad! He lists the corruptions of Israel—the politics, the priests, the prophets, the members. Read this chapter and it will visibly shake you. *ONE* major reason for God's punishments is the misuse and abuse of the Sabbath!

Now you and I both know Saturday ain't Sunday and the "Sabbath" ain't the Lord's Day! So don't get off on that. But there is a principle here—"No nation can disregard God's commandments without being punished." The Jew abused the Sabbath and Christians violate Sunday! We have decided it is our day—the "only day I have to . . . ."

So, God is "shutting her down!" He used the Arabs and turned off the oil! Gas stations close, tempers flare, inflation skyrockets, shortages occur, jobs fail, nerves fail—and we wonder *WHY?* Could God be telling us something?

We have neglected spiritual matters. Bible class and worship are avoided and neglected! God cannot and will not let us get by with it. Worship, family ties, spiritual matters belong to Sunday—the Lord's Day. It is *HIS DAY*—not *OURS!* God was angry in Ezekiel 22—He is likewise angry today. It is a shame and disgrace the way many selfishly abuse Sunday.

# "ON DEVOURING WIDOWS' HOUSES"

*"Woe unto you, scribes and Pharisees, hypocrites! for ye devour widows' houses."* Matthew 23:14

This verse has always "bugged" me . . . I still do not fully understand it. It is located in the middle of Jesus' most scathing sermon . . . it is not aimed at drunks, divorcees, or scalawags . . . it is listed with pretended worship ordinances . . . it is directed to church leaders. Whatever it is—it made Jesus mad! This can be done! All know how to get drunk—but how do you devour widows' houses? Especially church leaders! This is not vandalism or highway robbery.

Then one day a newspaper hit my desk . . . one of my best friends of long standing has been indicted on the misuse of trust funds. I am here not interested in the innocent-guilty aspect. I, personally, hope he is innocent. This is not the issue at this moment.

This article is interested in nailing down "devouring widows' houses" . . . the news item focuses on the real issue—our personal responsibility as public leaders to our members. Some preachers use their good name for commercial gain. All kinds of things are sold to a trusting clientele because the minister has a brotherhood reputation. Fund raisers must be careful! Using the preacher, elders, etc. funds are raised for silly causes! We have a sacred trust as leaders to protect the members! They give to something because we vouched for it!

Protect the innocent, the elderly, the widowed! Jesus won't like it if you don't!

# "EMOTION—INSTITUTION"

An intellectual was observing recently that religion and church could not get along. He said they were contradictory. Now he did have a point! Religion is individual; God has sons but no grandsons! Religion cannot be inherited. Religion is emotional—each man has his own convictions and feelings. Then this privilege is institutionalized—the form, traditions, and structure war against the individuality. In other words, personal freedom of worship is stagnated in corporate worship. As I said, there is a partial truth. Phariseeism destroys the spirit, for the letter. Corporate worship must also have spontaneity!

However, this fellow is wrong! He thinks religion must *always* be "adrift in personal feeling." He says groups, cells, churches destroy this! But religion is more than emotional, personal "mountain-top experiences." Apply this same logic to love and marriage! One can flit from one love to another—but marriage would ruin it. I am tired of celebrities recommending "relationships" as against "the sheet of paper (marriage)." It is now a proved statistic that relationships create more problems than marriages! Apply this same logic to country patriotism. Do you flit from one country to another? Who pays your board? Apply this to jobs. Do you flit from one to another? Or does someone have to "stay put"?

You see, religion is more than personal—it is communal! We are called as a group—the ekklesia! We must not let the group destroy the person—we must not let the person destroy the group.

# "SIGHT"

There are various means of sight—of seeing and knowing. Not to see in these various ways is blindness. How is your sight? Are you blind? There is nothing more frightening than blindness—nothing more helpless. What are the various ways of sight?

(1) *SIGHT.* Some cannot see what they are looking at! They are blind. Satan blinds us that we do not see. If the blind lead the blind, they fall! The usual excuse—"I just didn't see it." This causes accidents, yea tragedies. Some contend, "I just can't see it."

(2) *HINDSIGHT.* History serves its purpose. Men who do not learn from history are doomed to make its mistakes. We must be enlightened by the past. We can see well looking backwards. But hindsight must not become an albatross! Philippians 3 says, "Forget the things that are behind." One is blind to the future who lives only in the past.

(3) *INSIGHT.* This is wisdom, common sense, perception, observation. It is an invaluable tool! So few have it. I Timothy 5 tells of leaders without insight who harm the church. Insight sees tragedies that are not yet evident! Hebrews 5 tells how insight determines between good and evil.

(4) *FORESIGHT.* How blind we are to the future! Man must dream and dream big. A good golfer sees his shot before he swings! Hindsight plus insight equals foresight! Jesus said, "Lift up your eyes." Paul was pressing on the mark of the calling of Christ.

How is your sight?

# "THE FAT IS IN YOUR HEAD"

Charlie Shedd wrote a practical book, *The Fat Is In Your Head*. He affirmed, having lost 100 pounds, that weight loss was in the mind—the discipline. No one argues with him. We control our bodies with our minds.

But this is not the concern of this article. We are not talking about "body fat" but "mental fat." You can feel, see, and weigh "body fat" but not "mental fat." Paradoxically, many "health nuts" are not bothered about their minds! Minds, like bodies, can get out of shape. You can run, watch your diet, sleep, and make your body trim. But this actually does little with our physical appearance. Yet, few even admit mental deficiencies! A diet for the mind is as essential as one for the mouth.

You cannot eat candy, fats, not work out, and keep in physical shape. You cannot work out one day and have it last for a year! This is true mentally. Do you read? Regularly? What? Is it balanced? Is it tough? Does it anger? Does it make you think? How long has it been since you changed your mind on anything? Are you "fat" in your head? Are you "trim" in the head?

If it is true that "you are what you eat," then it is more true "you become what you think." Many fear a "soft heart." We should fear "a soft head and a hard heart." The most neglected area of public health is in the mind—not the body.

Are you in shape?

# "TAIN'T SO"

An alleged expert recently defined the church as "A hypochondriac widow living behind closed blinds with the memories of her dead husband." It is easy to make a whipping post of the church . . . if anything is wrong the church is handy to blame. There are things remiss in and with the church but with all its faults it beats anything else!

(1) The church is not a hypochondriac. Webster says, "morbid anxiety over one's own health." The church is a *giver* not a *taker;* the church is here to serve, not be served. The church is the mother of education, benevolence, and progress. The church cries over a world lost in sin. Tain't so!

(2) The church is not a widow—but an expectant bride. Paul uses such an illustration in Ephesians 5:22-29. In Revelations 21:2 the church is pictured as a bride adorned for her husband. All Christ left on earth is the church; this church is His body and glory. The church joyfully anticipates the coming Lord. Tain't so!

(3) The church is not behind blinds but out in the streets. The church is the salt that penetrates the world. The church does what nothing else can do. The church is not in politics and legislation; the church is saving men and making them Christ-like. Tain't so!

(4) The church does not remember a dead husband but worships a resurrected Lord. Jesus is now "King of Kings and Lord of Lords." He sits at the right hand of God. Tain't so!

## "BRILLIANT—BUT WITH NO SENSE"

Brethren confuse the IQ with wisdom, and brilliance with common sense. How tragic! Recently in a leading brotherhood journal an editor tried to explain brilliance. He said he tried to help a congregation accept "a preacher's brilliance." He said he failed and the church dwindled down to nothing.

But what is brilliance? If he is so brilliant why must someone assist his acceptance? He may be high in IQ but what about "people sense," common sense, wisdom? It takes practical wisdom to build a church. If a man is all that smart why cannot he know this? He may have a high IQ but he still "ain't got no sense"! So he is not so brilliant after all! A "book sense" may not be brilliant! Brilliance is the ability to "use what you got."

But to proceed further—this young man is carried away with his own brilliance. He "looks down upon" his brethren and laughs at their ignorance. He is "too good" to "waste time" with them. He is an intellectual snob! He resents the brethren for not following him and develops bitterness against them, the church, and life in general.

Then the church dwindles down to nothing and he writes sarcastic articles against them. He may be a master at satire but he needs spirituality. And brethren lament, "He is so brilliant!"

When are we going to learn?

## SOME THINGS THAT SEEM TO BE—AREN'T!!

At least that's what daddy always said! This is why wild-eyed liberals with progressive education and social welfare create chaos—it sounds good but it just won't work! Programs look great on paper but persons don't fit on paper. So many political and religious programs forget one little thing—*people!* That's why Jesus didn't mess with programs—He came to change people.

Now for instance—consider the 18 year olds! Logically, if one fights in war he should be allowed to vote, to drink, to be legally responsible, etc. It all sounds logical. So a few radical young people yelled—and TV, newspapers, and politicians heard the yells! And politicians want votes instead of righteousness . . . so they beamed their program to youth . . . work for us and we will let you vote! So they did! *18's* are now *21's!* The papers played up their "new freedom." Man, they are it!

But are they? What seems to be—ain't! A teenage girl (17) talked with me recently. This law affects her! She now doesn't wish to be 18! This is one of the great years a person has! Why? She doesn't want all this responsibility! She still wants to depend upon parents, church, and society! She sees her lack of wisdom and experience at *18* in handling life. *PARENTS,* our children need us at 18, 19, 20, yea *21!* We are pushing them into things they don't wish! Tell them *what* to believe; tell them *what* to do . . . down deep, they will appreciate it.

Some things that seem to be—*AREN'T!!*

# FREEDOM IS HARDER THAN SLAVERY

Of all the things wanted and fought for is freedom! Blood has been shed throughout time for freedom. "For freedom did Christ set us free." Saved men are free in Christ! Slavery is tragic! It really creates pity and disgust. Americans for years have been up-in-arms concerning our war prisoners. They were released within the year with great fan-fare (and justifiably so).

It has been interesting and heart-rending to follow their lives. Several have committed suicide; several have been divorced; several have been unable to adjust. This article is not in criticism of any P. O. W.!! Perish the thought! But it points out the price of freedom! Freedom demands . . . requires! It is easier to have someone think for you and regiment you than to really be free. It is easier to be a robot than a human.

This is also expressed by students at liberal colleges. For years they succeeded in removing rules—now dorms are cold, without chaperones. In a recent *Times,* following many upsetting results of such, the students were now asking for *rules* and *chaperones!* They see their folly.

It is easy to tell toddlers when to bathe, eat, etc. It is another thing to baptize teenagers into adult life—freedom. This is why some don't make it! *FREEDOM IS HARDER THAN SLAVERY!*

# WHY DO WE LOSE?

Neal Marshall will be the first to tell you I don't know anything about football. But to watch the Cowboys run "power right" three times and then fail at the two yard line . . . *WHY?* Tom Landry is a football genius . . . he is a football computer . . . but he failed and the game was lost. *WHY?* Did he wish to lose? It killed him! Did he not have other plays? Hundreds! *WHY?*

(1) *STUBBORNNESS.* Man in business, at home, in personal relationships, can become stubborn. *This is the way we are going to do it!* So we fail—and will not learn. We are going "power right" even if we lose! There is a thrill in "flat out running over people." We like it so we pursue it! Man has always fought change, innovation, alternatives, progress. This is the nature of man. Businessmen succeed—then destroy their own business. Politicians become bureaucrats. Churches stagnate, while re-living "the good ole days of yonder past."

(2) *BLINDNESS.* "Open thou mine eyes that I may see." It is very difficult for man to see himself. He would deny it if he did! Man has a very difficult time being honest. So he remains with the comfortable. It is heart-breaking to see churches and preachers who are blind to the real situation. So we are blind to new ideas, new methods, and new people. We refuse to learn. The solution becomes a problem. It is tragic to watch leaders calling plays who remotely don't even know what is going on! "If the blind lead the blind we will both fall into the pit."

## "HHH OR THE CROSS?"

Your editor watched in amazement as three USA Presidents attended the funeral of Senator Humphrey . . . a president in power, a president in limbo, and a president in exile . . . Carter, Ford, and Nixon. Three presidents as different as three men can possibly be—friends, enemies, different parties, love/hate feelings, all were visible in their presence. Not since 1961 and the funeral of Sam Rayburn had three presidents met. Past and present differences were transcended because a man had died.

This is a viable challenge to our brotherhood . . . If HHH could bring together three political antagonists, why cannot Jesus and the cross bring brethren together? What will it take? There are at least *27* factions (splits) in the restoration movement . . . there are liberals, conservatives, progressives, middle-of-the-roaders, rich, poor, ins-outs. Brethren change congregations over "personality clashes." Years later it is either sadly regretted or laughed about! What will it take? Cannot the cross of Christ bring us together? Cannot the cross transcend our human pettiness?

What will it take to teach us brotherly feelings, patience, understanding, kindness, longsuffering, forgiveness, and love? Why destroy ourselves over something that will be trivial within a few short years?

The power of HHH was good for politicians . . . the cross of Christ could be this for brethren.

# MAN IN THE IMAGE OF GOD

*"And God said, Let us make man in our image, in our likeness . . . So God created man in his own image, in the image of God created he him; male and female created he them."* Genesis 1:26, 27

We have always emphasized the dignity of man—that he was created in the image of God. Man was made "like" God. This has been accepted among brethren. But what does this mean? How is man "like" God? And if man is only "like" God how is man "unlike" God?

The *first* obvious fact is "man is not like God physically." This corrects many false concepts of God. God is not flesh, blood, and bones. God is spirit (John 4). God is not made of dust and cannot return to dust. God is described to man in "human terms"—these are called anthropomorphisms. But God is not man, and man is not God. God cannot be located, confined, or bound to time as man. So man, physically, is not made in the likeness of God.

*Secondly,* several differences cannot be bridged. God is creator; man is created. Some attributes of God are non-transferable—immutability, perfection, immortality, unity. Man can emulate but not attain. God is infinite and eternal; man is finite and mortal. God has a non-derived existence. He was not made nor born and cannot die. Man is both made and sustained—his very existence is totally derived and dependent.

This helps clarify the expression "made in the image of God."

# "MARRIAGE AND MONEY"

*"For the love of money is the root of all evil..."* 1 Timothy
6:10

Anyone who has been involved in marital counseling knows that a major issue is money. This is true the first year in marriage—and the 50th year in marriage. Money is always "in the top five" in marital tensions. All talk about, fuss about, misunderstand, and get hurt over money. It is always a source of irritation and alienation.

(1) Money is the battleground for other wars. Hurt, frustration, disappointment, anger, pride, guilt, love, etc. express themselves in the arena of money. So money often gets the blame when deeper issues are at stake. To solve money issues still does not resolve the real issue! The personal faults sometimes are evaded or avoided to argue over the tangible money! Money may be only the visible top of an iceberg!

(2) Money is a convenient way to express values, role expectations, and emotional needs. Paul says "the love of money"—not *money!* Money gets the blame—the problem is a deeper need in the heart. Some would buy friends and family with money. Others will go bankrupt—not because they cannot handle money—they cannot handle themselves. It is a great barometer of a man? If one can handle money, he can handle other facets of life! Men think, "provision is manliness." Others think "personal appeal" is determined by the bank account!

*MONEY*, who needs it? *I DO!*

# CROSSING BRIDGES AHEAD OF TIME

Man usually—and wisely—says, "I will not cross that bridge until I get there." This eliminates worry, fretting, and sleepless nights. Do not borrow tomorrow's troubles (Matthew 6:33-34). There is no need in crossing unnecessary bridges.

But there is another angle—some bridges can be crossed ahead of time! Turn to Mark 16—the women of Jesus came to anoint His body. The stone had been rolled aside for them by an angel! God had crossed the bridge ahead of time for them. Christians cross their bridges ahead of time! *HOW?*

*By the word of God!* David hid the Book in his heart that he might not sin (Psalms 119:11). Jesus rebuked Satan in the temptations with scripture. Scripture preparation allows us to cross bridges ahead of time!

*By character!* Strong, matured Christian character handles attitude and habit problems. There is no substitute for Christian maturity.

*By commitment!* One does not have to decide about each service he attends when he has made a total commitment. The same each Sunday on giving. Take your check already made out and you save "fumbling in your pocket."

*By the morning watch!* Time spent with God saves time! Makes time! Find God before you meet man. Solve your problems before you tackle others! Christians can cross bridges ahead of time!

> *"And, lo, I am with you always, even unto the end of the world"* (Matthew 28:20).

# "HEARING HEARERS"

It's easier to preach than to practice,
It's easier to say than to do;
Most sermons are heard by the many
But taken to heart by the few.

Jesus said, "Take heed *how* you hear," "Take heed *what* you hear," "He that hath ears to hear let him hear." Jesus had a great parable he titled, "The parable of the sower" (Matthew 13). Scholars also call this parable "The parable of the soils." There were four kinds of hearts—hard ground, weeds, shallow and good.

Do you listen? Do you apply lessons to others or yourself? Do you learn, or just re-enforce your prejudices? Are you changing? May I suggest four kinds of listeners?

*SPONGE*  A sponge soaks up both good and bad, and when pressured pours out all of it. A sponge withers, not grows.

*SANDGLASS*  This involves the old statement, "in one ear and out the other." There is nothing retained.

*STRAINER*  Some brethren strain out the good and keep the bad. Jesus said, "Ye strain out a gnat and swallow a camel."

*SIEVE*  A sieve strains out the chaff and gets the grain.

Are you a "hearing hearer"?

## "K A A"

*TEACHERS!?!* How wonderful they are! Your editor has been so richly blessed with knowing and having great teachers! Learning is exciting! To know Biblical truths, Biblical characters . . . yea God is wonderful! Praise God for faithful teachers . . . "and the things that thou hast heard of me among many witnesses, the same commit thou to faithful men, who shall be able to teach others also" (2 Timothy 2:2). I *MUST* grow as a teacher!?! *HOW!?!* The answer is KAA!!!

*K nowledge*—One cannot teach what he does not know anymore than he can return from where he ain't been! This is why I teach—to know and to grow! *READ! STUDY! PRAY!* Don't re-hash, or emphasize the familiar and prejudiced. Go from *MILK* to *MEAT.* Chew, agonize, probe the great principles of Christianity and of life.

*A ttitude*—The only commodity people follow is competency . . . study, prepare to be competent! However many cannot be teachers or soul winners because of their attitude. We are in the "People Business" not the "Book Business." IQ, talent, preparation cannot overcome a perverted attitude.

*A ction*—Teachers in Bible Classes are not teaching secular subjects. It matters not only *WHAT* you know but *WHO* you are! Teachers must *LEAD!* Teachers are *LEADERS!* Teaching is far more than "class presenting" . . .

*KAA!!!*

# "TRANSPLANTING RELIGION"

Psalm 137 is an interesting Psalm. It is a Psalm concerning the Jews taken to Babylon in captivity. "We hanged our harps upon the willows . . . How shall we sing the Lord's song in a strange land?"

The problem is "transplanting our religion." Many are religious at home—but the problem is to "take it with us." Many "faithful down on the farm" never identify when we "come to the big city." Some "city churches" do not make this easy—they are cold and unfriendly.

Others do not transplant their religion to college. Seniors graduate from high school then leave the church! Others do not transplant their religion in marriage. They attended faithfully until they married—then they quit. Some members work well with one preacher but when he leaves they never transplant their loyalty to the next.

One of the hardest transplants is from the "church building" to the job. Those who "pray" sometimes can also "cuss." Farmers have always told me "transplanting" is a difficult business. But pure religion can be easily transplanted because it is not based upon place, preacher, locale, age, etc.

Do you transplant yours?

## "THE FAILURES OF MAN"

In Burton Coffman's poignant book, *The Mystery of Redemption*, one learns there are three incurable and irrevocable areas of human insufficiency—ignorance, guilt, and mortality. Man walks down these blind alleys of frustration and bitterness. These obvious "flaws" will hound men to the judgment.

*IGNORANCE.* Man has learned many things—but he fancies he has learned everything. But the computer cannot contain even that—and when he solves one thing this creates millions of new problems. Even worse—man thinks he is smartest when denying God. Only ignorance could conclude that evil men have superior intelligence! Man is ignorant in all respects.

*GUILT.* Man is helpless—sin just won't "wash off." Perfume it, deny it, run from it, drown it in alcohol. Sin lies like a hot iron stamped in human conscience. Man is guilty as hell itself. Yet when admitting his greatest needs he denies his real problem—sin!

*DEATH.* Every town has a cemetery. Ultimately every doctor will lose every patient! The rich, powerful, educated, popular, loved—all meet death's appointment. It may be postponed a few days but not lifted. "It is appointed unto man once to die." Man stands defeated and helpless at the casket of death.

# "EXCUSES"

Read Luke 14:15-24 (frightening language). Jesus invited friends to His supper in this parable . . . with one consent they made excuse. You will never find a sinner without also an excuse!

(1) *EXCUSES ARE LIES!* "An excuse is a thin-skin of falsehood stretched tightly over a bald-faced lie." Can you imagine someone buying land sight unseen? un-tried animals? a Jewish man of that time henpecked? (women had no rights). Jesus says angrily, "none invited will be welcomed!" Notice the three excuses:

(2) *LAND—PRIDE OF POSSESSION.* Man takes snobbish pride in possessions. Man likes "toys" . . . this thing and that thing! So many brethren are unfaithful—they are too busy with their toys! People missed out on Jesus for toys (cars, hobbies, trips, etc.).

(3) *OXEN—TOO BUSY WITH BUSINESS.* Business, providing for your family, etc. are good—to a point. But some think they are indispensable to job, civic work! They give their money in substitute of themselves. A man too busy to worship and work for God is "too busy." Many brethren will miss heaven over job obligations! It ain't worth it!

(4) *WIFE—CLAIM OF LOYALTY.* The Great Command, Jesus said, is love God FIRST, TOTALLY, WITH PRIORITY! Some refuse baptism over a loyalty to Mother! Some will not attend because their mate is not a Christian! Others are not faithful because their children are not interested!

**BOY!! WAS JESUS MAD!!**

## "TOO HIGH A PRICE FOR A POINT"

Handball is a grueling game . . . I take pride in hustling. Run into the walls, slide on the floor, go at 110%! It sounds good and it is the American way! But an older player, not nearly as good, but who always beats me, told me one day, "There are some shots not worth going for . . . you must learn this . . . you pay too high a price for some points." When you make a point at the price of fatigue or injury the point is not worth it. You can make a point but lose the game!

Preachers should learn this! They will alienate themselves from the elders and maybe get fired, over trivia. Was the idea worth it? Was it worth the price?

Elders should learn this. There is a time to lead, but never to drive. Sometimes they use their "authority" only to alienate the church. Was it worth the price?

Children should learn this. They "finagle" parents for something but it back-fires! Was it worth the price?

Parents should learn this. They try to win all the battles with children. You can win all the battles and still lose the war . . . you can win all the arguments and still lose the game. Jesus taught in Luke 14 there is a time to negotiate . . . yea even lose . . . because in that loss you can win! Don't pay "too high a price for a point."

# "CHOICE AND VOICE"

Members do drop out of church. Members once dependable, yea great workers, do become frustrated and quit. Why? There must be an honest answer! Your author would like to list two:

(1) *CHOICE.* From the Garden of Eden man has been a "free moral agent." God allows Satan to tempt and man to choose. Man is a creature of choice. God does not coerce man —He does not force Himself upon man. This is called the "Humility of God." Consequently, there is a difference in "Leadership" and "Headship." Christ is "head" yet He "leads." Force, arm-twisting, driving are repugnant! Elders are to practice "leadership"; it is easier to fall into the rut of "headship." Members must have "choice." They must commit themselves. They must be "led" not "driven." Members choose—they must choose to work even when the "honeymoon period" is over!

(2) *VOICE.* There must be "feed-back." We call this a "breakdown in communication." It is true members should listen to elders—but it is equally true elders must listen to members! They must be *heard*. Members will never quit while progressing! Why do preachers quit? teachers? church workers? members? When they cannot see progress—or future. When their talents, thinking, and lives are unwanted! A man quits working before he quits attending. This is why leadership of necessity involves growth and accomplishment. When this ceases then members quit!

"CHOICE AND VOICE"

# "ENOUGH DIGS MAKE A GRAVE"

Last week two more preachers ceased preaching, to enter secular work. They were good men—excellent preachers— the brotherhood needed them. True, some need to quit! True, some have "quit preaching who remain in the pulpit." But these two were dedicated men!

Every week discouraged elders, deacons, Bible teachers, and church workers file through my office. Many just need an encouraging word—others either slack in their work or quit entirely. It is so unnecessary. Country people say, "Enough digs make a grave." The reasons given as to why various folk quit are always childish and little. But each was simply the "straw that broke the camel's back."

It is not the major problems—like standing for truth, or self sacrifice. It is those *"digs."* Not from "billy goats" but from leaders! You work, and push, and live, and give, only to be "shot down." When you find a good church worker or preacher, "stay off his back." Jabs, notes, cute statements, "put-on-the-spot" actions shrivel a man's soul. He gets to wondering "is it worth it?" Then after some unnecessary "broadside" he says, "You can have it."

He didn't want to quit; he will never forgive himself for quitting! But the "digs made a grave—for his soul." He lost spirit and heart. The brotherhood does not deserve some of these dedicated men! But, of course, the world never did! "Of whom the world was not worthy." Hebrews 11:38.

## "TOUCH??"

Years ago I visited a rest home with Jack Exum. Loveable, tender Jack! The lady being visited was aged and invalid, caused by a stroke. She was a pathetic sight . . . and her mouth could not contain its saliva. She was to a great degree senile. When we went in Jack reached over the rail and hugged her then kissed her. Her eyes gleamed with joy! Her day was made by Jack! I couldn't have done it! It is easier to visit "at a distance." Society is often bewildered at such!

Yet this is the phenomenal power of a touch! A new baby is brought to church and all rush over to see—but especially to touch! One way or another we will touch that baby! But we back away from the handicapped, the aged! Age diminishes the eye, the ear, the tongue, the mind—but not *the touch!* Old folks can still *feel* by *touch!*

Doctors can be kind simply by squeezing a hand; so many older people in homes need someone to "just hold their hand." They are so lonesome—they communicate by touch.

We need more "touch" at church! Do you make it a point to seek out and speak to the aged? Even more so do you have their name? And when they reach out a wrinkled hand do you hold it? They need to be hugged and kissed! It will make their day.

Jack Exum can do it—can you?

## NO SUCH THING AS A GOOD FARMER!!

You hear it said often down home, "He is a good farmer." We know what they mean—but it is not so! No man is a good farmer! He may be successful, rich, qualified, hard-working—but not good!

He may be good in cotton or good in corn or good with cattle. He may be good in sand or good in black land. He may be good in dry years or good in wet years. He may be good one year and a failure the next. Times change! Men good with a mule cannot handle a diesel. Men good with "40 acres" cannot handle "4000."

This is a vital lesson in life. Parents are not equally good every year! Parents may be good at various stages in child development. Parents may be better with one child than with another.

This is true with preachers. A preacher may be good at one church and a disaster at another. He may be better one year than another (even ball players do that). A preacher may be good at certain stages in a church's growth—just like parents with children. Teachers may be good on certain subjects at certain times.

Elders may be good in various ways. This is the idea of "group leadership." A great eldership results from a balance of good elders.

What am I trying to say?

# "COLOR ME COLOR"

Psychologists don't have anything to do but sit around and analyze the "nutty aspects" of man. One of these areas is the "Psychology of Clothes." Clothes do "make a man." Clothes are to be worn appropriate to the occasion. They add dignity or detract from the event. Bright or colorful clothes "lift a person"; dull and dark clothes depress.

Psychologists say depressed or problem people enter their offices in dark brown, black, or dark blue. One said he had never had a patient to come in red. Their clothes express their mood. Psychologists suggest part of the cure is to dress in color rather than in something depressing.

This explains some things! Preachers, psychologists say, are the most melancholy, suspicious, and pessimistic of all professionals. They invariably dress in black. Even morticians now are wearing colorful suits. Preachers and morticians have always kinda looked alike. Come to think of it—the more dull, drab, and blah the preacher, the blacker the suit! So we enter hospitals with their sick patients, and funeral homes with their grief dressed melancholy in black . . . it further depresses.

So, visit the sick and grieving with some color! Put some "life" into the visit. Don't make bad matters worse! Lighten the load; invigorate the hurt; apply the "flair" to heal.

You guessed it—I don't have a black suit. Paint me bright blue, red, green, polka dot! Man, I'm alive!

# "ON WEARING OVERALLS'

*"Indeed all of you should defer to one another and wear
the "overall" of humility in serving each other." 1 Peter
5:5 (Phillips).*

Your author was raised in a cotton patch—he never knew
anything but "overalls" until high school—then he graduated
into "blue jeans." Folk laugh about "pore country ways" but
"overalls" and "blue denim" have just about cornered the
fashion market! Proud, rich society folk now forsake the tux
for the overall. Kinda amusing in a way.

Christians need to wear their "overalls." Peter says this
is humility—the every day element in Christian living. It is
easy on occasions to wear humility—but Peter goes to the
market, to the school, to the home—talking about life, not
"dress-up" occasions. Humility never divided a church;
humility never "cut a brother down"; humility never "forced
its way."

Peter was there, in John 13. James and John (with their
mommy) had jumped ahead of the others, wanting the
special seats next to Jesus. This really irked the others so
they argued over which one was the greatest. Peter chimed in
to Jesus saying he could never deny him. This looked like
"Romper Room" on TV for 2 year olds. So Jesus put on "his
overalls" and picked up a towel to wash feet!

This attitude, and dress, builds churches! This attitude
serves! This attitude makes *BIG* men! This attitude is
unaware of "who gets the credit." Are you wearing your
"overalls"? Not the blue-denim! The ones made of humility.

# PUBLIC SUCCESS AND PRIVATE FAILURE

Elmer Prout wrote a thought-provoking article recently concerning Noah. All are thrilled with his building the ark, and the flood . . . but we kinda wish God hadn't told us about his getting drunk! We like our heroes perfect! Noah condemned a sinful world, built patiently an ark to specifications, and saved his family . . . then he got drunk! It just doesn't fit into our human thinking! Success is no preventive to future temptation. Many stand with the large, then stumble over the small. Salvation is not one monumental decision—it is a life of faith.

Then there is another character in the story—the son Ham! He saw Noah's drunkenness and nakedness, so he ran to tell it! Whether he was upset, angered, or tickled the Bible does not say—but he had to tell it. There is too much being told in our brotherhood today. Noah was drunk, yes! Noah had sinned, yes! But telling it did no one good! Of the many choices Ham had he chose the worst. Why do you tell what you tell? "It's the truth" is not a sufficient reason to talk!

But the other sons, Shem and Japheth, tried to restore. They did not gossip further . . . they did not make "bad matters worse." They walked in backwards, not looking, and covered up the "sleep-drunken Noah." They didn't even peek! The fact of getting drunk was not changed but Noah was given opportunity not to be disgraced. Canaan, the son of Ham was cursed.

Isn't the Bible an interesting book?

# "A PRO—THE VANISHING AMERICAN"

Youth fascinates me! Instant success, acceptance, stardom! Upon the first obstacle failure and bitterness come. Youth has some excellent ideas worthy of support but they demand *all* their interviews be adopted *now.* People come into the church then face disillusionment! Why? They demand perfection immediately.

It takes time to make a *pro!* A *pro* starts in the "back room," on the "low rung," as an apprentice. He learns his trade backwards and forwards; he learns who he is and how it happens. He does his craft with a pride and satisfaction. Dreams do not come true because they ought to but they are caused to. A *pro* is disciplined and self-managed. He pays the price to be respected in his field. There is no shortcut to glory—there is the tedious pain of a "pro."

Every preacher should be a *pro.* He should pay the price in study and work. He should know God, the Bible, people, and the situation. He should always be prepared; he should never stop studying and growing and doing. This demands a dedication and work schedule that sometimes dismays. Yet a *pro* has satisfaction which cannot be taken away.

Yet the irony! The preacher should be a *pro* without becoming "a professional."

## "AM I BALD?"

A man, after years of wearing a moustache, shaved it off. To his surprise and consternation few even noticed! This proves people do not "look at us" like we think they do! It has been said we would not even recognize ourselves walking down the street if it were not for our clothes.

Someone has a scar, big ears, wrinkles, baldness, etc.! They usually think this is all people see. When you know a person, love a person, accept a person, these are not seen. Even the color of one's skin is forgotten! Yet toupees, cosmetics, body developers, sell like crazy. We have the idea if we change a flaw the world will applaud! But the world is unaware of the flaw to begin with! Others see a total personality—not a flaw!

The tragic yet true fact is that people are not thinking about you—they are thinking about themselves! So we imagine and worry and fret and make matters worse. Why ruin a life for the sake of a flaw? If they don't like you "fat" would they like you "thin"?

You see—the real flaw is self—personality—character. We worry endlessly and spend a small fortune to "look attractive" when this time and money should be better spent on personality. You don't have to be grouchy, temperamental, loud, rude, mean, shabby. But personality will show—even through cosmetics! A really beautiful person shows through ugliness and handicap! *We can all be beautiful!*

Which returns me to our question, "Am I bald?"

# "THE SIN OF BOREDOM"

America's unique sin is boredom. Well known people even commit suicide in the name of boredom . . . the boredom of interstate highways . . . the boredom of assembly lines . . . the boredom of old age homes . . . the boredom of living! Pornography, violence, and crime feed on boredom. Marriages, jobs, friendships are destroyed by boredom!

A well-known psychologist thought boredom came from coercion, but many like Paul, in jail, were not bored. Another thought it was "structure hunger" but one can be bored by structure itself. Psychology has now decided boredom is "An incomplete striving for meaning." Boredom is meaninglessness! Boredom is not apathy—an accepted lack of meaning. So boredom is meaninglessness, not monotony. Knitting and mowing yards are monotony, but many enjoy them! In tests, people have preferred work to no work. So it is not work that's boring, per se.

It is tragic to find some Christians bored! So many are. To them Christianity, the church, yea even life have all lost meaning. Church is attended on Sunday, with nothing given, nothing expected, and nothing gained. We return home bored. Some members are driving themselves crazy boating, going off on weekends, etc., seeking something to eliminate boredom. Their recreation becomes equally as boring!

We must die to live; we must die to reproduce! We must return to soul winning! We must return to the real meaning of Jesus. Can you imagine the Apostle Paul bored? even in prison? Can you imagine the early church bored? Persecuted —*YES*—but not bored!

Boredom indicates meaninglessness—a Christian cannot have that!

# "GOD'S GYMNASIUM"

*"For bodily exercise profiteth little: but godliness is profitable unto all things, having promise of the life that now is, and of that which is to come."* 1 Timothy 4:8

The Oympics of 1980 are already in the news . . . football has begun . . . sports is the "opiate of our modern people." Jogging and exercises are popular. Americans are health conscious—physically. But God has a gymnasium—one given to the training of godliness. Let's look at his program.

(1) A disgust of sin. As one develops godliness, he is more and more shocked, repelled, and disgusted with sin. Doctors hate disease; Christians hate sin! Sin destroys godliness; godliness destroys sin. Hatred of sin is a signal of growth !

(2) A hunger for the word . . . the sincere milk of the word, hungering and thirsting for righteousness, a craving to know God in His Son! A sheep that won't eat is sick! How is your appetite?

(3) A desire to change and to grow. To win "gold" medals in the Olympics requires years of dedication. What a price winners pay! Christians change their lifestyle to develop Christ in their lives. The "bottom line" is "changed and maturing Christians." God develops only one thing—Christian people.

(4) A love for others. There is fraternity among athletes. A common respect and interest. Brethren love brethren; brethren wish to share Christ with others. Have you signed up at God's "Gym and Trim"? *Exercise unto godliness!*

## "THE FAILURE OF SUCCESS"

Positive Mental Attitude (PMA) is the order of our day! SUCCESS . . . SUCCESS . . . SUCCESS. We must WIN—WIN —WIN! Even down at the church. Brethren are pushed to "the breaking point." "Winning is everything," is seemingly our philosophy. So we drive ourselves, feel guilty with ourselves, then blame God with the setbacks.

This must be corrected! God has never asked anyone to succeed—but He has demanded faithfulness. At random times Abraham, Jacob, David, Moses, the prophets, Peter, and Paul have all been in the throes of defeat. At last encounter there were *187* books on *Success,* and *How to Be a Winner* present in our stores! So far as I could find—not one book on "How to Be a Failure."

There is valuable power in positive thinking; we are not to develop a loser complex. But all of us do fail—at various times we all taste defeat! Things are not perfect; we are not perfect. Many of the greatest principles of life are learned through suffering. Man learns more from failure than success.

So I read the "How-To" books, hear the "success" tapes! One thing is obvious—these persons are hiding behind "success" rather than being honest with themselves and and objective in life! The "Success Syndrome" is idolatry! It is a refusal to be honest; it is another facet of being "phony."

Be honest with yourself; be yourself! Do not try to make life what it is not; do not try to be what you are not!

# "FOUR WORDS THAT RHYME"

*DARE!* Life is a risk! To be a "dare-devil" and "to dare" are two different things. A wee baby attempts to walk! A man with a dream changes the face of the earth. Men who dare are ridiculed, fought against, then immortalized. Columbus dared discover America. Ira North dared to build Madison Church! We need men who think *BIG* and act *BOLD!* The church has been hurt more by "staying put" than by error! *DARE!*

*CARE!* Several times in the gospels a word is used, but only in reference to Jesus, "being moved by compassion." Jesus cared! Preachers can say anything they will as long as brethren know they care. Jesus cried over Jerusalem; He wept at the grave of Lazarus. Paul cried over Israel; he remembered the poor.

*SHARE!* People who *DARE* and *CARE, SHARE!* The opposite of pride is not humility but gratitude. Gratitude is the mother of humility. Grateful men are generous givers. Americans—brethren—are so prosperous! We waste more than people in other nations earn. We must share—both our Christ and our abundance.

*BEAR!* Read Galatians 6. Christians should bear the burdens of others! There is no fellowship on earth like that of the church! The strong remember the weak! The rich remember the poor! The old lead the young.

> Four great words that rhyme—
> Are they found where you worship?

## "ANOTHER COP-OUT???"

*"That which was from the beginning, which we have heard,
which we have seen with our eyes, which we have looked
upon, and our hands have handled, of the word of life."*
1 John 1:1

There are all kinds of excuses! One is more "deception"
than excuse! We are quite critical of the twelve apostles! How
dare Peter, James, and John go to sleep in Gethsemenae?
Why couldn't they understand? Why did they fail so miser-
ably? Why there is no excuse! They saw Jesus! They heard
the Sermon on the Mount! They watched most of the great
miracles! How dare anyone not believe! "Why, if I had been
*one* of the twelve . . ." Believing must have come easily!
"Why, I would have been an elder, preacher, song leader,
Bible teacher, soul winner!" This is just another modern
cop-out!

Have you considered the difficulty they had in believing!
Can God be handled in flesh? localized? Jesus had to: be
toilet trained, learn to walk and talk, grow up physically! He
had all the human body limitations. Did he snore? have bad
breath? sweat and smell? get tired, hungry, and thirsty. He
was so ordinary—poor, a carpenter's son, from Nazareth, the
stigma of a scandalous birth, uneducated. How hard it must
have been to see such a Jewish man and say, "This is God!"
Jesus was patient with them.

"Jesus saith unto him, Thomas, because thou hast seen
me, thou hast believed: blessed are they that have not seen,
and yet have believed." (John 20:29)

There is no place nor time for a faith "cop-out."

## BEING THE RIGHT PERSON IN MARRIAGE

Some succinct, accurate, yea brutal things are oft times said about married people. "They deserve each other." "What does she see in him?" "I don't know why he married her." "You gotta be kidding!" "I feel sorry for her being married to him." "He really has a cross to bear." Yet these statements touch a pulse-beat in marriage . . . Fantasy says "*find* the right person to marry" . . . a princess, a beauty, a rich widow. Find this fantastic person who will make you "live happily ever after." Marriages built upon fantasy are misery. Divorce becomes the *FIRST*—not the *LAST* resort! Some even have the idea "I deserve something better—I deserve happiness." This is why American marriage is in trouble.

But realism says "*be* the right person." Suppose I did "find the right person!" Would I deserve her/him? Why should the "right person" want you? You want the *BEST*—but are *you* the *BEST?* Marriage offers responsibilities! There is no "right persons"; there is only "rightness between persons." This article does not encourage the lowering of romantic aims; on the contrary—be the *BEST*, accept nothing in marriage but the *BEST!*

So again, the problem in marriage is *people!* People fail—not marriage. The solution to marriage is still people. Bad, sickly, carnal people cannot build a happy Christian home. Our breakdown in marriage is a breakdown with people! So build matured people—the "bottom line" is still "changed" people.

# "SPOILED ROTTEN!"

*Fourteen* chocolate pies in *six* days! This is the record during the Greenville meeting! Each day a special gift was delivered to my motel room—a flower arrangement, basket of fruit, knick-knacks, recipes of the Ladies' Class, and a candle made like a hunk of cheese. This was so refreshing and motivating. It is no wonder the members came around to personally introduce themselves. Noon sermons had a meal—inviting town workers to come and *hear* and *eat!* One had *135* present. These noon services *MADE* the meeting! I became acquainted—so many "fellow employees" were introduced to the church! Attendance records were made and *ten* responded to the invitation. You are going to hear great things from this church! Watch 'em grow!

*Why?* Because of hospitality, thoughtfulness, unselfishness. A preacher is either a "Somebody" or a "Nobody"! If he is not a "somebody" why invite him to preach a meeting? No, he is not God—he is not to be elevated to angelic posture. But this attitude of "Let him get by like I do" is both negative and resentful. If members will not be hospitable to a guest preacher they will not be to themselves and to outsiders! Christians are commanded to be hospitable; a qualification of elders is "lover of hospitality." Great churches are hospitable churches. Paul loved Philippi "because they sent time and time again." Your preacher does not wish charity—he is not on welfare . . . but their hospitality was inspiring and will never be forgotten! It made a better preacher of me! Let's "spoil each other rotten" (Romans 12:10-13).

# "TO TV OR NOT TV"

NASA recently spent $213 million getting TV to isolated villages in India. Seems they were "missing something in life," not having TV. Is the best TV no TV? . . . That is the question? Did they miss something? Did these Indians need TV more than jobs, wells, bathrooms, yea some bare necessities in life? Which of these would you choose? Don't tell me!

TV changes people; TV is dangerous, addictive, sedating . . . it affects your mind. It can make a slave of you. You must use it without harming yourself. The average time watching? 7½ hours per day in the winter and 5½ in the summer. That is too much anything except prayer, work, Bible Study, doing good. TV fills a vacuum—a need—otherwise these hours would not be expended. Our children have watched 15,000-20,000 hours of TV by the time they graduate from high school.

TV goes to the mind. It does things to people's heads. TV develops the right side of the brain rather than the left. Thinking people are "left-handed" in development. So TV controls the non-sequential, non-analytic thought. Watching, to a degree, becomes brainwashing.

So since TV is here we must determine how we will use it—or it will use us! TV affects our perception of the world. Some rules:

(1)  First be a Christian. Be selective.
(2)  Limit your time. Don't let TV become a monster.
(3)  Pay attention to what TV has done and is doing to you.
(4)  Take care of your "mind" (Romans 12:1, 2).

## "SAINTS AND SNOBS"

*". . . When thou makest a dinner or a supper, call not thy
friends, nor thy brothers, neither thy kinsmen, nor thy
rich neighbors; lest they also bid thee again . . . but when
thou makest a feast, call the poor, the maimed, the lame,
the blind.*
*And thou shall be blessed; for they cannot recompense
thee, for thou shall be recompensed at the resurrection of
the just."* Luke 14:12, 13.

Snobs at church? People who attend but who feel they
are rejected? Are there "Ins" and "outs" at church? Is our
greatest feeling rejection? Are brethren "lonely" at church?
Our text is frightening!

This article does not apply to those "Back Seat Members" who slip in and out stating, "Leave me Out!" That's
their problem. This article also does not apply to those who
quit the church if a problem comes. The church cannot help
those who refuse help.

But the article does apply to those who come, yet do not
feel accepted, wanted, involved, or blessed! Read on . . .

(1) Do you think you are friendly because you speak
warmly to your clique . . . when is the last time you spoke to
a guest or new member? Try sitting at a new place in worship.

(2) The church, in practice, really has no place for the
single, the handicapped, the poor, the misfit, the widowed,
the divorced, the failure. They are treated as "lepers." Their
names may be on the roll, but they don't really "belong." To
be among the "Outs" at church is terrible!

## "SELLING PAINT—SAVING SOULS!"

Recently, in a conversation at a Lions' Club meeting, a highly successful paint salesman gave the *THREE* keys necessary to sell paint:

(1)  The prospects have to like you.
(2)  Your price must be in line (consistent).
(3)  Service.

This sells paint . . . but he went further. The key—the primary factor is No. 1—people must like you. This is crucial . . . people will not buy from anyone they dislike! Soul winners must know how to be *friends* before they can be soul winners! Soul winners are first "friend makers." Trust must be cultivated. Seed is not sown on highways but in carefully prepared soil! Prospects must be cultivated before sales are made.

He then went even further . . . No. 1 can be linked to either No. 2 or No. 3. You must have No. 1! No. 2 and No. 3 fail but No. 1 and No. 2 or No. 1 and No. 3 will work! To have all *3* is dynamic success!

This is equally true in soul winning. People want consistency—they do not like petty little church squabbles. They will buy consistency in life! They will not buy our private hobbies!

Finally, people expect service! We are *servants.* We baptize, then lose the babes in Christ! Remember—the seed is always in the fruit! Peaches sell themselves—not just the naked peach seed. These things sell paint. These things will save souls!

# "AREN'T YOU GLAD . . .?"

(An outline based on an article written by my good friend
  Bob Mize.)

I. *THAT YOU CANNOT KNOW THE FUTURE.* Man
has always been fascinated with the future. The rage today is
the seer, the prophet, the horoscope. All read Jean Dixon. All
should want foresight, but not foreknowledge. Man could not
withstand such august knowledge—knowing the day his
parents would die, a friend would turn against him, etc.!
Jesus says, "Each day has enough trouble" (Matthew 6:33,
34). Man cannot carry that load of a yesterday gone and a
tomorrow that may never come. Knowing tomorrow would
be sheer horror!

II. *THAT YOU CANNOT READ PEOPLE'S MINDS.*
My boys watch the "Amazing Kreskin" on TV—a mentalist.
He does amazing things picking people's minds; yet invariably
he asks of his audience, "What is your name?" A man doesn't
know much about others if he doesn't even know their
names! Jesus said of certain truth, "You cannot bear it now."

III. *THAT YOU DON'T HEAR ALL THAT OTHERS
SPEAK ABOUT YOU.* Talking about others is usually bad or
stupid because it is seldom objective and knowledgeable. It
is usually an evaluation, good or bad, built from feelings, not
facts. It is humorous sometimes what people say about our
lives—things both unreal and unreasonable. Such knowledge
would put us in bed.

IV. *THAT ALL ARE NOT ALIKE.* At random times we
have wished we were someone else. That is a bad practice.
After all is said and done we are usually glad we are ourselves! Who would you wish to be? Aren't you glad you
aren't me?

# "GRACE BUILDERS"

A third grader prayed a cute, incisive prayer, "Thank you for those I like and those I don't like!" She may have been young but she already knew there were "problem people," unlovely, obnoxious, rude, hard to get along with, demoralizing! John the Apostle had his Diotrephes. You mention a certain congregation to one who knows—a little laugh comes—then the "Billy goat" there is discussed!

Critics, "church policemen," know-it-alls . . . we just don't prepare preachers, elders, deacons, teachers, church workers, for these folks! They keep classes upset, give elders ulcers, run off preachers, and demoralize church workers! We run out of "cope." "We get tired of the hassle." So preachers leave! It is never as many as five who run the preacher off! The preacher leaves with one comment, "There are a lot of good people there?"

What do you do with such people? Shoot them? Of course not! They are "Grace Builders." Every church has *one* or *more*—they make you study harder and pray more! They make you grow up in spirituality (maturity). In the long run they do more for your growth than sweet people! They keep you from being proud and comfortable—they keep you on your toes.

No, Hodge cannot get along with everyone! He is glad God has not commanded him to "like" everyone! Since he is not perfect he does not even claim to "love" everyone! He cannot handle all conflicts; he does not even know all the questions, let alone the answers! In fact, he is probably the main "Grace Builder" for others!

# ONE DEAD CIVIC CLUB!

People are people—whether in the church or in the civic club. 2 + 2 = 4 both in church or in the civic club. We need to learn this! "People savvy" is true just like gravity. Truth has no respect of persons.

There is a particular civic club—your author has spoken there off and on for over 15 years! They have been dead/are dead/will continue to be dead. Some nice, lovely guys doing just one thing—getting older. The District Governor was asked the reason. His answer, "The club was endowed by a well-intentioned member." They have no projects—they have it made! *THEY ARE DEAD!* A civic club without good works is a contradiction!

Then one day it dawned on me—this is how most churches would like to be! Let a millionaire pay our bills—hire a few talented men to do *OUR* work! Of all things "get the church out of debt!"

The worst thing that can happen to a church is to get out of debt! Like Laodicea, "we have need of nothing." The bills are paid and we are "at ease in Zion."

Abraham refused to have the Cave of Machpelah given to him—he bought it! David refused to sacrifice to God that which cost him nothing. Comfortable sermons, little programs, and easy living all fail! "God, keep us on our toes!" *BETTER,* "God, keep us on our knees!"

# "SUPER BOWL MANIA" REFLECTIONS

The world can now "go back to work"—"to normalcy"—"Super Bowl Sunday has come and gone." This author has spent as much time on the ball courts as anyone—he profoundly loves sports—he even admits to being taken with "Super Bowl fever." Herein are some observations:

(1) *THE GOOD.* This could only happen in the USA! We are truly people with personal liberty! Communist athletes are molded into robots—athletics is a profession. The joy of victory and the pain of defeat are brainwashed from their personalities! Sports is an agonizing job—a performance! Only in the USA could such a stupendous event stop the nation—whose outcome has no *significance* at all!

(2) *THE BAD.* This could only happen in the USA! We are truly people without discipline . . . self indulgent and abusive of our freedom! $300 million gambled on a game! Some ventured their life savings—with millions living in poverty and starvation, some still spent a small fortune on one "Super Weekend." Excess . . . silliness . . . an insult to maturity and responsibility! What an image for the world to see of us! The score is not remembered tomorrow!!! Idiotic nonsense . . . no wonder the games are always disappointing!

(3) *THE OTHER.* Our teens and pre-teens were not captured by all this as were adults! Teens even went outside to shoot basketball goals! How dare them in such a "life-or-death shoot-out." Grownups do not have the simple perspective of youth . . . the youth for which games are made.

(4) *THE CONSOLATION!!* It only happens once a year!

# AS SIMPLE AS 1-2-3

*"But seek ye first the Kingdom of God, and His righteousness; and all these things shall be added unto you. Take therefore no thought for the morrow; for the morrow shall take thought for the things of itself. Sufficient unto the day is the evil thereof."* Matthew 6:33-34

As simple as *1-2-3!* All of us have a "worry" problem! It may be less or more in some of us but nonetheless it is there. Worry, according to Jesus, is pagan; worry is little faith; worry is sin. To many, it is the "respectable" sin. We all commit it, yet have little regret about it. Others are frustrated.

While visiting a hospital recently a person was heard to remark, "Nearly every person on the psychiatric ward is a member of the Church of Christ." Well, this is exaggerated—but it contains an element of truth. What is the answer to negative worry and positive fear?

It is as simple as *1-2-3!* There are only *three* days in a man's life—yesterday, today, and tomorrow. Man can only live *one* day at a time—*today*. He cannot be involved with the grudges of yesterday and the fears of tomorrow and live as he should today. Paul forgot the past; we must keep a hope in the future. We should face today with confidence.

As another has said, "Man, like the bridge, was designed to carry the load of the moment, not the combined weight of a year at once."

As simple as *1-2-3!*

# "ROMANTIC LOVE NONSENSE"

Herbert G. Zerof has written an interesting book, *FINDING INTIMACY*. His job was to explode the myth, fantasy, and wishful thinking of "romantic love." Life and love are not fairy tales . . . we do not "live happily ever after." Real life is not a permanent exciting weekend, an enduring vacation to the South Seas. Too many approach life and marriage with unrealistic expectations. Only after all of this is exploded can real love or true intimacy be found. Real love means the abandoning of the imagined mystique of romantic love.

Real love requires character. Marriage does not fail—people fail. Real love involves "giving" more than "getting." Singles often think "marriage is the answer to all problems." It is not; it can make bad matters worse. Many marry, subconsciously demanding that the mate fulfill all their needs and wants. This is disaster. Partners must not be expected to give us everything we have missed in life.

Real love is compassion and understanding. Yet no one person will ever understand himself, let alone someone else. The other person must be given space, freedom, time alone—yea, each of us must be encouraged to develop as a person. Love is not a mind reader! Love's mystique preaches this! Quit playing games and having disapppointments! Tell your mate your thoughts and feelings. Openness is necessary for true intimacy. Even with disagreement the other's self esteem and worth is reinforced. Trust, love, demonstration result in intimacy—an enduring intimacy.

# "EXERCISE"*

*"But refuse profane and old wives' fables, and exercise thyself rather unto godliness. For bodily exercise profiteth little; but godliness is profitable unto all things, having promise of the life that now is, and of that which is to come."* 1 Timothy 4:7,8.

Since bodily exercise profits little—it takes a "whole lot to do any good." This is our excuse for playing ball, etc. But there is correlation in bodily exercise and spiritual exercise. A "Charles Atlas" type was asked the key to his shape. His answer was simple:

(1) Find any program that is reasonable—the exact program is not the main thing—*BEGIN TODAY! RIGHT NOW! THIS MINUTE!* What a mouthful! We are going to start dieting—after Christmas, start jogging next week—but we never do! Do you need to be baptized? Do it today! You wish to begin Bible studying, praying, visiting—*START TODAY!* Don't "wait until next year." *START TODAY!* This is the way to eliminate the negative and accentuate the positive.

(2) *Keep at it!!!!* Some join the YMCA—kill themselves the first trip then never return! You cannot go when convenient—on sunny days—when you feel like it. Once you start skipping you have had it. Job "worshipped God continually." To do something regularly, consistently—this is discipline! In Christian living the regular heartbeat is better than the spasm—and the steady pull counts for more than the spurt. "Shape up or ship out."

*From Joe Barnett

## "ON SHAKING OFF DUST"

*"And whosoever shall not receive you, nor hear your words, when ye depart out of that house or city, shake off the dust of your feet. Verily I say unto you, it shall be more tolerable for the land of Sodom and Gomorrah in the day of judgment, than for that city."* Matthew 10: 14-15

This is another familiar maxim of Jesus! Yet so misunderstood! We enjoy "kicking off the dust." A "righteous indignation" consumes us when a cottage meeting is rejected or stopped . . . when prospects "drop out." Like Maude in TV, "God will get you for that." It is kinda, "look what you're going to get for what you did to me!" The imagery does come from Jews coming to Jerusalem via Samaria. They were to "kick off the pollution" before entering Jerusalem.

However, the "dust" is not to "curse" others! It is not "washing blood off our hands." This "dust" is for *our* benefit—not *theirs!* Jesus says "Keep negative factors from your mind." If a man rejects the gospel—don't you quit! Don't let that bother you as you knock the next door! Kick the dust off! Don't let it bother you! Leave failure on that doorstep and proceed as if it did not happen!

How many Christians do you know that have been zealous for over ten continuous years? How many have become only "bench warmers"? They allowed failure, discouragement, disappointment, ill treatment, false goals, etc. to build, build and build. Now they are negative, cynical, and sour! They should have "kicked the dust off."

Be positive this year!

## "IT'S HARDER TO GO DOWNHILL"

It has been months now since knee surgery . . . it's about time for some more sympathy (and chocolate pies). This cranky old knee done taught me something . . . I can walk without a limp even race upstairs . . . but I cannot walk down steps normally or naturally . . . the harder I try the worse it is! That taught me something—it is harder to go downhill!

It was proved at a football game! I watched people climing up and down stairs. There is "weight" involved in climbing but "danger" in descending. It was harder to go downhill! As a boy this would not have been believed! It was always easier to ride a bike downhill than uphill! Mountain climbing never looked easy to a country boy!

And it is not easy! But it is still easier to "go up" a mountain than "climb down." It is not dangerous to lose speed going up a mountain but it is to gain speed coming down!

It is difficult to go from "the bottom to the top," but it is really heartbreaking to go from "the top to the bottom." It is hard to accept second place! It is hard to admit you can no longer do well what you once did! It is hard to take a back seat or a smaller church. It is hard to get whipped in a game by a man once not your equal. Getting to the top ruins many, but going to the bottom can ruin those good enough to have been on top.

My ole knee knows.

# "COLUMBUS LECTURES"

This "Ole Country Boy" recently visited the Central Ohio Lectures at Columbus. Five churches have five simultaneous meetings with the five preachers making the five-church circuit. This was quite a different experience . . . new, unique. Some observations:

(1) All 5 churches are different. Even as individuals they have distinct personalities. This is good! We try to force all Christians, all congregations into one mold. This explains why some churches and preachers don't fit. This could mean that neither the preacher nor the congregation were evil! They just didn't fit! Some preachers try to go in and remold congregations . . . some congregations try to change the preacher. Let each congregation and each preacher and each member be themselves! Corinth was different from Athens! What works at one place explodes at another! Each congregation must analyze its own area and membership and then formulate its own program! Quit trying to be a Broadway or a Madison or a Garnett Road. *BE YOURSELF!*

(2) Such an arrangement provokes judging . . . which of the *five* preachers were best! The five preachers constantly asked, "Which church did you enjoy most?" Kinda juvenile! All churches were the *GREATEST* and all were the *WORST!* Each had strengths and weaknesses. This is like asking, "Which of my children is best?" We must outgrow such! All churches must evaluate their own weaknesses and fortify their strengths. *WE ARE ALL GOD'S CHURCHES AND GOD'S CHILDREN!* All *FIVE* churches are scriptural! All *FIVE* preachers are scriptural! Different—yes?!?! Valuable—yes?!?!

# "THREE DIMENSIONS IN GROWTH"

"*. . . after I have been there, I must also see Rome.*" Acts
19:21.

"*. . . be of good cheer, Paul: for as thou hast testified of me
in Jerusalem, so must those bear witness also at Rome.*"
Acts 23:11.

Paul wanted to see Rome—He saw Rome! What are the
fundamentals guaranteeing success?

(1) *DESIRE!* Paul, from a jail, had "missionary goals."
His past sacrifices were insufficient for his soul. He wanted to
preach in Rome, then go on to Spain (Romans 15). Great
churches begin with great dreams! There must be the goal
before the reality. The *seven* great revivals in the OT were
begun in the hearts of *seven* men! Not to have, suggests
failure in desires! Sometimes we think we desire when it is
only wishful thinking!

(2) *DEDICATION!* Paul dedicated himself to his desires
(Romans 9, 10). There was no price he would not pay. He
did not "count the cost—he paid the price." All churches
wish for improved attendance, contribution, and baptisms!
Or do they? Is this the goal in their lives. Our dedication
exposes our real desires.

(3) *DETERMINATION!* Paul was like a bulldog. A jail-
house could not discourage him. So many desire and dedicate
—yet quit in disillusionment! Paul was a "canner" not a
"can'ter" (Philippians 4:13). He refused to quit!

The church today can grow! It must grow! Desire, dedication, and determination will do it!

# "RE-STUDYING FAMILIAR VERSES"

*"Train up a child in the way he should go: and when he is old, he will not depart from it."* Proverbs 22:6

All of us know and love this verse; all of us have been deeply troubled by it! It sounds simple and easy. Rear children correctly and they will always be faithful. It is all "cut and dried." Yet is it? Many great parents tried hard, only to lose a child or children! They blame themselves! They think they failed. Parents can fail—TRUE—but remember "God is the Father" in Luke 15 of the Prodigal Son. Did God fail as a parent? I think not! The Bible teaches "free will" as well as determinism! Some scripture overrules or makes exceptions to other scriptures! We tend to forget this. We pull out *ONE SCRIPTURE* and make the whole world fit it!

Also, Proverbs 22:6 states a principle, not a law! There are exceptions to general statements. *AGAIN,* the promise not to depart is when "they are old," not "when young." But the verse still haunts.

Flavil Yeakley, Jr. offers an observation relative to translation. He suggests, "Train up a child 'in his own way' and when he is old." In other words, Solomon is saying permissiveness in youth will be hard to correct when old. Now this is opposite to our traditional or familiar view. Will you automatically reject the *NEW* for the *OLD?* Is this Biblical honesty? Will you study the matter further? Is it a closed book? It bothers us when people alter our "pets" doesn't it? I don't know what translation is right. I do know permissiveness is wrong! A spoiled child will have difficulty being a matured adult. I also know some great parents carry guilt which is not theirs. Study for yourselves.

# "STRANGE BEDFELLOWS"

*"Mercy and truth are met together; righteousness and peace have kissed each other."* Psalm 85:10.

Truth is never in any extreme; truth is never in the "middle-of-the-road" between extremes; truth is in *both* extremes! This is a vital key to life, negotiation, and progress. *PARADOX* is what some call it! Tall and short, hot and cold, flowers and weeds, love and hate, fear and courage, empty and full, fast and slow, grace and law, zeal and knowledge . . . *BALANCE!!!* Christianity is balance. One must be *RIGHT!* But *only* to be interested in *RIGHT* leaves one in a fight, feud, and war all the time. The circle of fellowship gets smaller and smaller; distrust, suspicion, and disfellowship result.

On the other hand interest *only* in *MERCY* empties the jails and creates chaos! We need scholars to study and soul winners to save. *WE NEED BOTH!* PhD's usually are not soul winners, but soul winners must also develop scholarship and Biblical knowledge. There is a place for all (1 Corinthians 12; Ephesians 4). One can be both *RIGHT* and *KIND!* Courtesy is a part of truth.

(1)  They *SHOULD* go together!
(2)  They *MUST* go together!
(3)  They *DO* go together!

Mercy and truth met in Christ! They did not *CHEAT*, but *COMPLIMENTED* each other. Obey Christ today!

# READING BUT NOT LEARNING

The Prince of Granada was sentenced to Madrid's old and infamous prison, the Place of Skulls, in fear he might aspire to the throne. For *33* years he remained in solitary confinement with but one book to read—the Bible. He read the Bible hundreds of times, but what did he learn?

There are 3,538,483 letters in the Bible.
The word, "girl," occurs once in the Bible.
No word or name of more than 6 syllables can be found in
    the Bible.
The middle verse of the Bible is Psalms 97:8.
The 9th verse of Esther 8 is the longest verse.

How tragic! An educated man with unlimited time studying the eternal book! He read but he did not learn! He did not learn how to be saved; he never had grace nor forgiveness; he never knew Jesus as Lord nor God as Father. All that time and labor to know only a few facts of curiosity. He read but did not learn.

Are we making the same mistake? Do we read through our own cliches and jargon? Do we know about God but not God? Are we interested in speculating about revelation but not saving our neighbor? Do we attend worship to hear comforting assurances rather than probing and challenging questions?

Are we reading and not learning?

# "HOW THE BLIND SEE"

In Syracuse we visited an interesting couple—a blind couple from birth with two babies—one 2 years old and the other 2 weeks (both can see). How can 2 blind people care for 2 wiggling kids who can see? Everything was in place in the house and the babies were clean and corrected. It was very impressive. Since my hobby is dog psychology I was quite interested in their "seeing-eye dogs."

(1) Dogs improve and obey with praise. Many dogs have been ruined by excessive correction and scolding. Dogs really love praise. It is amazing to learn all the things the dogs learn and do! I got the name of their obedience school—now if I can just get the deacons to go! You cannot demoralize the dog! Then, from pride, the dog strives to do better the next trip than the one before.

(2) The dogs know their master. The man took his wife's dog to show that he would not obey him, but gladly would her! Christians ought to remember who their master is! Jesus is Lord! We don't fit the harness of Satan.

(3) This man recently responded at the services. His statement, "Spiritually, I have been walking by *sight* and not by *faith*." A blind man is walking by sight! How incongruous! But does not this indict us all? Are we not walking by sight? How many of us are walking by faith? *FAITH!* It takes faith to be out on the public streets blind, led only by a dog! That's faith! To put your life into the hands of a dog! But Christians have God—and we walk by *faith* and not by *sight!*

# "THE BROADNESS OF THE NARROW WAY"

*"Because strait is the gate, and narrow is the way, which leadeth unto life, and few there be that find it."* Matthew 7:14

Our text is true—Jesus said so. But this has become "our main text"! Hopelessness, frustration, fear are the result! Men are too discouraged even to try. Many are afraid to act since they may make a mistake and "be struck dead like Uzzah." Since most have "goofed" they have concluded they are "past redemption."

We need to also observe the "broadness" in the narrow way:

I. The narrow way is still "broad enough for everyone." Jesus died not only for the church but for the whole world! Wake up! There is no sin too powerful for the blood! There is no sinner "too far gone" to be saved! This is the hope and power of the gospel! *YOU* can be saved! White-black, rich-poor, good-bad, successful-failures! There is plenty of room for *ALL* in the narrow way!

II. The narrow way is "broad enough for individual differences." No one man, or party spirit, or pet peeve is in control! God does not accept whom we accept nor reject whom we reject! The narrow way is not a religious straight jacket! A narrow way does not mean a "narrow mind." Men make God's narrow way more narrow than He intended! We have rejected men He accepts! To be narrow is not to conform.

III. The narrow way is "broad enough to allow all to hold the hand of Jesus." He can reach us all; we all have access to Him. There are no distinctions in Christ. He is interested in our "biggies"; He is also interested in our trivia. Don't ever forget the "broadness in the narrow way."

# "PUBLIC PRAYER"

Public prayer leading is an awesome responsibility! The entire congregation is wishing to worship and talk with God! Jesus condemned egotistical prayers of show! There must be a "balance" with the one praying! Public prayers inspire or bore—they lead or disgust. They are vital! Here are some points to ponder:

(1) *ORGANIZE*. Jesus prayed an "organized" prayer in Matthew 6:9-13. This is a model, an outline, a manner. If a sermon is to be prepared, why not a public prayer? If a preacher needs an outline to speak to men, why is it wrong to have an outline to speak to God? What about the sick, immediate church needs, special requests. Neither sermons nor prayers should come "off of the top of our heads."

(2) *BE SPECIFIC*. A dismissal should be a dismissal, a prayer for the sick should be for the sick. Prayers at the Lord's Table should be just that.

(3) *BE HEARD*. Prayer is "to God" but it is a collective, not a private prayer. How can others *AMEN!* a mumble or a silence? It is a shame that men give so little thought and preparation to public prayer.

(4) *BE SHORT*. Prayer can be too long! It is better to be short than long. Members become restless and disgusted. The model prayer was short and to the point.

(5) *INSPIRE*. Do you draw the audience to God or repel them? This is the crux of the matter. *PRAY* to God! Help others pray to God!

# "SEATTLE SLEW"

*"And he beheld them, and said, what is this then that is written, The stone which the builders rejected, the same is become the head of the corner."* Luke 20:17

Seattle Slew won the Triple Crown—the Kentucky Derby, the Preakness, Belmont! All America idolized this 3-year old horse! But not the pros—the experts. Eddie Arcaro is one of the great jockeys of all time . . . quiet, knowledgeable, usually a good commentator. But even his bias showed! He kept "rapping" Seattle Slew as mediocre. But all the horse did was win, win, win!

This is the mistake many "pros" make! Not amateurs! You see, Seattle Slew, in horse circles, is an outsider. He was not owned by the "horse people"—the Whitneys or Vanderbilts. He had no "horse pedigree." So the "horse pros" said it was the wrong horse, the wrong jockey, and the wrong game plan! But the horse won, and won, and won!

This same mistake was made over Christ! He, religiously, was an "outsider" . . . He didn't come from the right city, family, and way. He was rejected, criticized, and crucified . . . by the "pros," not by the public! This was caused by "professional pride," yea religious arrogance! Seattle Slew will never be accepted by the "horse set" . . . Jesus Christ will never be accepted by the proud.

## "PRACTICE KEEPS PERFECT"

*PRACTICE!* What all hate to do! Let's "play the game" rather than practice. A great pianist said, "If I don't practice a day, I know it; if I don't practice for two days, the critics know it; and if I don't practice for a week, the crowd knows it!" *PRACTICE!* All of us know "Practice makes perfect." All know that one practices to get to the top. But few realize one must practice to "stay at the top." It takes more practice to "keep you there" than it took to "get you there."

*NOTICE!* Airlines several times yearly send their best pilots for intensive training. This teaches awareness, while eliminating bad habits! Surgeons must constantly "practice," else their quickness of hand eludes them! Proficiency is kept only with constant practice. Athletes make blisters practicing for hours. When you watch an artist doing something "effortlessly" you know "much effort" was spent.

The lesson? Once great preachers, are not anymore . . . they stopped studying and growing. They are coasting. Great elders of one decade can destroy their efforts the next decade. Great Bible teachers (with great hurt) must now be ousted. They ceased to practice. Bible study requires practice . . . prayer requires practice . . . right attitudes demand practice!

Are you a "Practicing Christian"?

# "GOING TO THE BIRDS"

*"Behold the* BIRDS *of the air: for they sow not, neither do they reap, nor gather into barns: yet* your *heavenly Father feedeth them. Are ye not much better than they?* Jesus in Matthew 6:26.

*BIRDS!* I am indebted to Dick Marcear for the following statistics. There are *4* billion *people* on earth—*100* billion *birds!* This is 25 to 1! Man will be *8* billion by the year 2000 —the bird population is constant. Perhaps they could take over the world, as a movie suggested! Another sobering statistic—if all the birds were destroyed, mankind would be devoured by insects within 30 minutes! God created an orderly, balanced world!

Again, man's heart beat is 72 times per minute—a bird's 1000! He constantly moves—hyperactive. Man eats 3 times daily, a dog once, a fish twice per week. A bird eats constantly! He never stops! The statement, "She eats like a bird," may mean the opposite from what it is intended! Yet God feeds the birds! 100 billion birds are constantly fed!

Notice, "your Father"—not, "their Father." They are but His *CREATURES!* We are His *CHILDREN!* Worry, fear, defeat, murmuring should never be named among us! God knows and God cares for His children!

"Are ye not much better than they?" Believe in God!

# "KNOWING TOO MUCH MAKES YOU KNOW TOO LITTLE"

*"Is not this the carpenter, the son of Mary, the brother of James, and Joseph, and of Jude and Simon? And are not his sisters here with us? And they were offended at him. But Jesus said unto them, A prophet is not without honor, but in his own country, and among his own kin, and in his own house."* Mark 6:3-4.

How tragic—God in the flesh in His home town—rejected! Jesus could do no mighty work there! *Why?* Because they knew too much!! They did not deny the wisdom nor the miracle! But they denied Jesus! *Why?* Because he was a local carpenter boy and they knew his family. Now what they knew was true. He was a carpenter. God in the flesh at a trade is within itself extremely fascinating. He was a Son of Mary—he did have brothers and sisters. They knew Jesus well—too well—they were too close! They couldn't see the forest for the trees!

But I am not worried about these "neighbors of 1900 years ago" . . . they are dead and gone. What about us? Are we making the same mistake. Someone mentions "Jesus." Our answer—"O, I know about Him." We know all that can be known—so what's the big deal? Mention the church, baptism, religion and people answer rather bored, "O, I know about that." So we today make the same mistake.

We are too proud of our knowledge and decisions. Oft times when something new is introduced, well-intentioned brethren are startled, "I never thought of that before," as if they knew it all. Some even deny it could be right since they hadn't heard it before! So they, too, deny Jesus. "Knowing too much can make you grow too little." Don't ever stop learning and growing.

## THE BIBLE'S UNKNOWN SOLDIER (PREACHER)

America has a renowned tomb to the "unknown soldier";
nearly every nation has. The Bible has an unknown preacher:
"With him we are sending the brother who is famous among
all the churches for his preaching of the gospel." *RSV*—2
Corinthians 8:18.

This is a very arresting verse! (1) It teaches that we
preachers can be famous! This was a preacher brethren loved
and respected. His praise was far and near! The brotherhood
has always needed great preachers! This man received a great
compliment—"famous for his preaching." (2) But the brother
is unnamed! Great character is even better than a great name.
A name can be inherited; character is earned. Paul does not
argue the validity of this man's fame! Rather, he congratu-
lates it!

Who was he? Why is he not named? Titus is named in
the context. There was no mention of persecution fear. Who
was he? Some suggest *one* of the four gospel authors. Others
suggest Luke, Barnabas, or Silas. Other lesser known men
have been suggested. But no one knows.

Who was he? Why is he unnamed? Was Paul jealous? Paul
had his faults but jealousy does not seem to be one of them!
He praised him! The readers knew *who* he was, as much as if
he had been named.

The "Unknown Soldier (Preacher)." A great lesson! The
church is still built by men who in one way are famous—yet
in another way remain anonymous. So be yourself for God
and serve God—whether you become famous or not.

## ON BOOK WRITING & PEOPLE

Book writing, otherwise called authoring, ain't all it seems to be—glamour, riches, acclaim—very few receive this, and they usually write the worst stuff. Thought-out, thought-provoking material doesn't sell—at least that's why mine don't! But some of the reactions border on the humorous.

My publisher called saying a buyer had returned a book because of one statement—one sentence. The buyer demanded a refund. The statement wasn't all that earth shattering and bad—the fellow didn't even go so far as to deny it. But the publisher had to refund the buyer 75 cents and that ruined his day!

But a tremendous lesson is involved! This buyer doesn't know what books are for! Any book has at least one statement you dislike or disagree with. In fact some of the greatest books have the most such statements. Any provocative book sometimes will even make you angry. But you don't send back a book for one sentence, paragraph, or page!

Again, the same is true of people. We try to "return people" for a refund because of one incident, statement, habit, or annoyance! And the fellow who actually helps us the most may jab us the most. Why let one trivial episode ruin a friendship? Books ain't perfect and neither are people! Wake up and use your noggin!

By the way, have you bought one of my books lately?

# "WHY WORRY?"

*"The legs of the stork are long, and the legs of the duck are short. You cannot shorten the legs of the stork, nor can you lengthen the legs of the duck. Why worry?"*
<br>Chinese Proverb

Why worry? Insurance companies get rich betting against your worries. Most things worried about never happen. Worry never solved a problem. What were you worried about this time last year? Why worry?

I. People worry because of hurt or disappointment. Shattered dreams or the successes of others deeply bother us. It is hard to accept our lot in life. We try to be other than what we are.

II. People want other than what is. When it is rainy we desire sun; when it is hot we desire to be cool. Making speeches finds me among the rich. Invariably as you wish their lot, they say, "I wish I could make a speech like that."

III. Selfishness, self-centeredness. "Get your mind off yourself and yourself off your mind." In this vein "self-help" books sometimes do more harm than good.

IV. Hypocrisy. We compromise, sell out our conscience, betray! This causes worry. Man must arrive with conviction and stand therein.

V. A lack of faith. Worry is doubt, not faith. Faith is God in our eyes. Why worry?

# "SCRUPLES"

A word belonging to my childhood. A great compliment to a man, "He has scruples," a "scrupulous person." You don't hear this mentioned much now—nor do you find many such persons. A little research found two fascinating things:

(1) The word, "scruple," originally meant *1/24th* of an ounce. An ounce is a small measurement—but 1/24th of that? How minute and careful could you get? To have "scruples" meant minute exactness! Men are careless today especially regarding religion. Seemingly detail is denied. Jesus said in Matthew 23 they should tithe the mint, anise, and cummin! It is not wrong to "strain out gnats!" The mistake is "swallowing camels." We need to know *what* we believe and why—even down to minute detail.

(2) The word also came from "a small stone in a man's shoe." Even the smallest of rocks ruins feet. There is pain with every step. A man with "scruples" invites pain others cannot have nor understand! Conscience does bother. We wonder what is "ought," and if we did right. There is pain involved in finding the right then doing it. It is hard to know *what* to preach and *when* and *where* and *how!* You always "second-guess" in failure. So misery can accompany the "scrupulous."

But it is still worth the price. You got any "scruples"?

## THE GREATEST THING I EVER SAW!

Your editor has had profound privileges in his ministry . . . great blessings. But the greatest was last Sunday, April 21st. He watched Brother and Sister R. W. Hartin of Cedar Hill sign deeds giving their farm to Medina Children's Home and the Dallas Home for the Aged (value at the present—$500,000.00). I have seen larger gifts and "bigger deals" but nothing like this.

Brother and Sister Hartin are "dirt farmers" who still "farm" on their farm. They are so modest in their living—still in the old 2-story un-airconditioned house. No frills—nothing fancy. You would never pick them out as among the rich! Their farm just happens to be in a fast-growing suburb and is worth a gold mine. They are living as if the worth of land had not changed! So they give away the "home place."

But the staggering aspect! They have seven children—all with modest means who not only did not try to sabotage this gift—they were thrilled with it! All seven children were present, with deep pride. They stood with us guests while giving their parents a standing ovation! Seven kids—all Christians, and all thrilled with their parents giving away the "home place."

Brother and Sister R. W. Hartin really know how to "raise kids." Wonder if the Hodge kids will "turn out" like this? What about yours? Is the church in your will? Would you give your "home place" to God? This was the greatest thing I ever saw! I'm glad my kids saw it!

# "DON'T BELIEVE EVERYTHING YOU READ"

Someone said, "Don't believe everything you hear!" TRUE! Will Rogers said, "All I know is what I read in the papers." *TIME* has "egg all over its face." In a pictorial report in its September 4, 1978, issue *TIME* magazine incorrectly labeled Cullen Davis in a picture. To further complicate matters the restaurant was given as "CooCoo's" rather than "Coco's." These errors are funny . . . but they point out some things:

(1) "Get the facts, man, get the facts." The reporter did not do his homework. The report was beneath professional dignity. When reporting—print the truth. This requires sweaty leg-work.

(2) Because something is printed does not make it so. ACU recently was slandered by lazy, incompetent dishonest journalism. A retraction days later on the back page does not correct the injustice.

(3) The *TIME* reporter showed his prejudice . . . he concluded his article with a "swat at Cowtown." He was not reporting a story but circulating a prejudice.

(4) *THE LESSON!* Why do Christians encourage "Brotherhood Watchdogs" to print papers assailing preachers, congregations, or projects with facts not checked out! Why do we wish to believe the worst? Why do we suspect conspiracy? The *TIME* fellow was wrong—it showed. So are scandal sheets among us.

# "ARE YOU A GOOD LISTENER?"

*"Take heed how, what, you hear."* Mark 4:24

God is awfully interested in our *hearing!* The Jews heard yet did not hear! Christ was crucified. Many think they hear when actually they do not. *NOTICE!!* There are different kinds of listening:

(1) *SOME LISTEN TO CRITICIZE.* They can "pick the speaker" apart! They hear "errors" but not "truth." And the one mistake made forced them to reject the entire lesson.

(2) *SOME LISTEN IN RESENTMENT.* They hear with hate. Hostility grows. The truth did not change their intellect but fired their passions.

(3) *SOME LISTEN IN SUPERIORITY.* This is snobbery in its worst. "I have no need of his speech—but from politeness and humor I will listen." "He cannot teach me anything because he is stupid."

(4) *SOME LISTEN IN INDIFFENCE.* How can people hear sermons for 50 years without being baptized? They listen in indifference. But how can you listen Sunday after Sunday without changing your ways? You are making the same mistake. You are like the man with a hearing aid who turns it off as he likes.

(5) *SOME LISTEN ONLY TO ANSWER.* They are not thinking objectively about an argument proposed but about their prejudiced answer! We encourage our guy to win but do not hear the opponent. This is not only rude but borders upon dishonesty.

(6) *SOME LISTEN TO LEARN.* They are seeking, knocking, asking. These people will be baptized, repent of their flaws, and grow rapidly. They are blessed because they are "Good Listeners."

# "MORE ON LISTENING"

Man is a great talker but a poor listener! The Bible warns so much about abuses of the tongue—and of the ears! Are you a good listener? ". . . let every man be swift to hear, slow to speak" (James 1:19). "When you see someone overeager to speak, there will be more hope for a fool than for him" (Proverbs 29:20). "To answer a question before you have heard it out is both stupid and insulting" (Proverbs 18:13). Do you just talk—or listen?

(1) Listening gives importance to the speaker. It is much easier to speak of the importance of an individual than to practice it by listening to him. Do you listen to your mate, your children, the poor, the inferior? To whom do you listen? Anyone?

(2) Actually most of us do not listen even when we are not talking . . . we are still hearing our own echo . . . thinking more about our answer. Fools are proud of their quick answers, not having listened (Proverbs 15:23).

(3) Do you look the talker in the eye and really give him your ear and consideration? Or is it that you are a captive audience anxious to walk away? To listen carefully is to give yourself to someone.

(4) Listening is the key to understanding. The Hebrew word for "obey" is the word "to hear." Listening is not grudging silence; it is not just "allowing him his turn," it is more than silence when another speaks! It is listening to learn, change, obey, and live.

Are you a good listener?

# "STRONG WILL VERSUS SELF WILL"

Sydney J. Harris, in his syndicated column, made a succinct observation, "the two terms, 'strong willed,' and 'self willed,' are contradictory yet usually considered synonymous." Our wills are our problem; much is said of the mind and feelings but little is said of our will! The crux of life is still the will! This is our failure!

*Notice!* Many parents complain (some brag) that their children are "strong-willed" . . . they will not go to church, do right, etc.! Such children are not "strong-willed" but "self-willed." In fact, such people have no "will" at all. They are driven by the appetites of the moment! This is our problem! Priorities, values, and godliness are lost to selfish pursuits. Most excuse themselves saying, "I cannot help myself."

Jesus had a "strong will"—He refused to knuckle under to any pressure. He had a one-track mind . . . to do the will of God. Nothing prevented His doing that! He preached "self denial" . . . a "strong will" over a "self will."

A "strong will" can postpone satisfaction, cope with frustration, and accept the limitations of reality. A strong will does not do what it wants to do, but what has to be done. Appetites overrule a "self will"; a "strong will" controls appetites.

"Self-willed" people are their own worst enemies! Yet no one can aid them—they become more "strong-willed."

# "SUCCESSFUL FAILURES"

Man in his pride fears failure! To be inadequate, to be inferior, is frightening! Man refuses to try lest he fail. Revelation 21:8 begins "Hell's Hall of Fame" with *"Fear."* But we all fail! We fail if we refuse to try! To some degree we are all "great failures."

Most great men of God were failures! None were perfect . . . Abraham, Moses, David, Samuel (his sons), Peter, John Mark . . . the list goes on. All at one time or another were failures! A man is not a "Failure Failure" *IF:*

(1) *HE KEEPS TRYING.* Peter who *denied* also *preached!* John Mark came back! Christianity is not the "one who falls" but the one "who keeps getting up." I need Peter—he failed, yet he succeeded!

(2) *HE DISCOVERS WHY HE FAILED.* This is self-discovery. Most of us fail where we think not! Moses sinned in meekness! Peter *sank* when *walking* on water. To know why is an insight into self. We can profit from mistakes!

(3) *HE LEARNS DISCIPLINE.* Discipline is a hard master. Peter a "rock"? The friends laughed—Peter even flinched! But impulsive, impetuous Peter became "rock." Failure teaches discipline.

(4) *HE DEEPENS HIS FAITH IN GOD.* James says trials are to be welcomed because they are blessed. Real faith, true patience comes in adversity and setback. Be careful about praying for patience! You may be slapped down!

Are you a "Failure Failure" or a "Successful Failure"?

# "WHAT LANGUAGE DO YOU SPEAK?!?"

When Peter denied Christ, his Galilean drawl betrayed him. People can be located by their speech. In *My Fair Lady* an Englishman could be located within a few blocks of his rearing! Try to hide an Irishman! Notice the foreign futility when speaking another's tongue. Rebels do not like Yankees —the New England sound. We all enjoy the Southern drawl of Tennessee, Alabama, or Georgia.

This is equally true in religion. We are not to use the "Language of Ashdod." Preachers are not pastors, reverends, etc. But we must probe deeper. Most of our communication, via print, TV, or radio finds "church of Christ people using church of Christ language being heard only by church of Christ people." We are stereotyped by our jargon! Our very language isolates us. What was intended as evangelism did not turn out that way.

But to go into our own personal lives and daily activities. What language do you speak? kindness or rudeness? patience or harshness? hope or bitterness? mercy or condemnation? magnanimity or pettiness? positive or negative? spiritual or worldly? love or hate? From the heart the mouth speaks! One of the greatest "X-rays of the soul" is the tongue. James says "sweet and bitter" cannot come from the same mouth. Jesus said "by our words" we would be saved or damned! The tongue is an unruly evil. What language do you speak?

# "THE ELUSIVE HOLY GRAIL"

In centuries past knights with great courage, blind faith, and questionable sense set out to find the "Holy Grail." Their faith assumed that this possession would solve *all* of life's problems—poverty, inflation, war, divorce, delinquency, and unhappiness. Generations gave their lifetimes to this quest . . . but they never found it.

But what would have been different if they had? Would peace have reigned? Would problems and war have ceased? Would men have changed? Is the answer to life bound in a cup or a bottle? Should we still seek for the grail? Of course not! Yet, man still believes in his private "Holy Grail." Money, education, success, travel, getting married, getting divorced, having children, children leaving, etc.! What is your "Holy Grail?" What would solve your problems and guarantee bliss for you? Is it in possessions? things? pursuits? Or is happiness an "inside job." Is the "Holy Grail" within?

This author enjoys being with millionaires. He really observes them. At the present those he knows are pessimistic, fearful, cynical—yea, miserable. They "found their Holy Grail." But it was empty.

As a boy, down on the farm at the Byrd Store, any man would have thought $100 weekly was a "Holy Grail." Man, that was "pie in the sky." But we all thought life on $100 a week would be like that of a king! But now we make much more than $100 weekly! And our Holy Grail is found to be empty!

Folks, "it ain't what you got but who you are." "Be content with what you have but not with who you are."

# "TO LIE OR NOT TO LIE—"

Down on the farm the question concerning cackling hens, "Is she laying or lying?" If there is anything universally found, it is lies and liars! Hell will be the home for "all liars" (Revelation 21:8). Parents, spouses, police—all seek to know when someone is telling the truth or lying. There have been all kinds of devices, gadgets, lie detectors. Now we have the ultimate—HS/2—a "Voice Stress Analyzer." They cost $1500.00 but competition will soon force the price down to $500.00. Attached to your telephone (with red and green lights) it will automatically tell you when the speaker is lying.

Now every church ought to have several of those (possibly 1,000 per church). Think of all the ways they could be used! When a person started to gossip, the "red light for lying" would come on—the gossiper could then be stoned in front of the entire church! Think how this excitement would increase attendance! Imagine how many "red lights" would go on when brethren sang "Jesus Is All the World to Me." It would blow out all the electric circuits. Preachers would immediately know who was innocent or guilty when he was counseling. A preacher could sit in his office gleefully listening to members lying to him via the phone!

Reckon this equipment would make people honest? Of course not—honesty is "who you are," not what an "HS/2" machine says about you.

## "ON HATING SIN AND LOVING SINNERS"

It is one simple fact that Christians are to *hate* sin yet *love* sinners! So simple to preach yet so difficult to practice. It appears contradictory. Some preach against sin so heatedly they cannot accept or love a sinner . . . others accept and love sinners to the degree they cannot preach against sin!!! *BOTH* attitudes are wrong! "After having preached like you did against sin, I don't see how you could associate with sinner X!!!" But I can! I must! We must hate sin while loving sinners! There is no contradiction, compromise, or softness involved.

To illustrate . . . I hate cancer but love cancer patients! There is no contradiction in this! Even if their cancer was basically "self-caused." Even if cigarette smoking caused the lung cancer the patient is still loved, aided, prayed for, served! Lung cancer patients must not be "shot" because we preach against cigarettes! Booze can cause cirrhosis of the liver but the patient must still be loved with compassion. Gluttony can cause stomach disorders; worry can cause ulcers. The point is vividly this—illness is hated but sick people are loved!

Compassion, urgency, ministry, encouragement must be given to the sick! They have priority . . . Jesus Christ calls the sick—not the righteous! "Go ye and learn what this meaneth, I will have mercy and not sacrifice."

I hate divorce but not the divorced! I hate drink but not the drunk! I hate sin but not the sinner! What about you?

## "TO THE STRONG? GRATITUDE!"

The opposite of *PRIDE* is not *HUMILITY*—it is *GRAT-ITUDE!* Gratitude dispels pride and produces humility. As a people we are suspicious of power, success, money, and talent. We are afraid of strength—we have all kinds of programs for the weak but none for the strong. Strong people have problems and weaknesses, too! Paul had a thorn in the flesh. Tragically, the strong that do handle so many things well, often make the mistake of thinking they can handle everything! This provoked Paul's "thorn."

What do the strong need? *GRATITUDE!*

(1) *GRATITUDE* is one's response to God! Our strengths are not our own personal attainments. Whether from birth, accident, or advantage all our talents and successes came from God! We are not "self-made men." Are we quick to forget? Do we really thank God for our country, homes, education, food, etc.? Or do we think it is ours by right? Wake up—brethren!

(2) Every sermon, as Karl Barth said, should begin with grace. Too often we tell people what to do, as it were, holding back candy as reward! God gave to produce repentance (2 Corinthians 7). We do not become perfect to demand grace! The grace is there, first!

(3) *REMEMBER!* What? The warning of Jesus, "To whom much is given, of him much shall be required."

*GRATITUDE!!*

# "THE UNCHURCHED"

Religion is again popular; youth openly talk about the Bible. God has become a *FORCE* again in life. However, 80 million—80 million!!!—Americans never "darken a church house door." No claim of religion. They are not atheists—they are not criminals—they just "don't go to church." *TIME* magazine looked into this—here are their findings as to *WHY!*

(1) *BURNED OUT.* Some tried religion—worked at it—got hurt, then quit. Religion is now met with cynicism and despair.

(2) *LOCKED OUT.* Some think a *SIN* or a *MISTAKE* or poverty or something makes them unwanted and out of place —the divorced, the failure, the prodigal all feel "out of place."

(3) *NOMADS.* One fifth of America moves yearly. Friends are made, then "good-byes" come hard. Upon moving, these nomads determine not to get involved with anyone. "Bedroom" towns find many citizens non-interested in any civic or public matter.

(4) *PILGRIMS.* Some people are always searching . . . always thinking "lightning will strike." They go from fad to fad . . . yoga, tongue-speaking, meditation, groups, cells, but not a simple church with a simple life.

(5) *CRITICS.* Last and least. They know what's wrong" with church members. The major complaint, "church members drink."

# "A DAY—NOT AN HOUR"

*"Remember the sabbath day, to keep it holy . . ."* Exodus 20

We really do need to *LISTEN*—to *THINK*—to *CHANGE!*
We need to *CHANGE* our concepts about the "Old Bible"
(Testament). Many have concluded that since the "Old Law"
was nailed to the cross the entire Old Testament was!
*ABSURD!* Some of us seem to think that the Bible begins
with Acts 2. There is a reluctance even to study the Old Testament. Principles and concepts are dismissed, "But that's in
the Old Bible." Truth is truth! The "Old Bible" is the word
of God, too!

We need to *THINK!* Medicine is worthless in a bottle—
it has to be taken! We have reduced Christianity to "going to
church." "Are my kids going to church?" "I went to church
five times in a row but my baby still got sick." Christianity
is not magic; you don't "go to church to go to church."
*THINK! WAKE-UP!* Church attendance is not a "protective
umbrella." It is not "religious insurance."

We really do need to *LISTEN!* God said, "Remember the
sabbath *DAY." DAY*—not *HOUR!* God said religious health
involved a *DAY!* A *DAY* that was different, uniquely holy
(set aside for God). A *DAY* for re-creation, not selfishness.
A *DAY* of rest, not frantic go-go-go activity. A *DAY* for
renewal, appraisal, priority evaluation! Just "running in to
partake of the Lord's Supper" is not what is *SAID!* This is
why *heaven* is called *sabbath!* One *DAY* a week to order and
prepare our lives, so that heaven can be ours! *LISTEN—
THINK—CHANGE!*

# "MAN—THE UNFINISHED"

Philosophers have long attempted to describe man—"The rational animal, problem-solving animal, the self-conscious animal, the talking animal, etc." Your writer cares little for the "animal" ending. He is interested in the fact that man is "unfinished."

(1) Animals are "finished." Dogs are dogs and cats are cats! Good and evil are not open to them. They cannot transcend their instinct. A dog cannot become a cat nor a cat a cow! They are locked in. Animals have a nature but man has a history. This means there is actually "no such a thing" as human nature! This is an excuse—a cop-out!

(2) Man is not evolving! Animals are not—man is not! This does not infer that man is getting better or worse. Man can destroy himself and he—by himself—cannot save himself.

(3) "Unfinished" means freedom—choice, direction, destiny. Man can elevate himself or destroy himself. We can become "like Jesus" or "like those who killed him." Man is a creature of choice. Throughout history man has known something is missing—that someone is God! Jesus told Nicodemus that he "must be born again." Man can be touched, man can repent, man can live for God! Man, unfinished now, can be later complete in Christ.

## "HAPPINESS"

What *ALL* desire and *FEW* have! Happiness cannot be directly pursued—this is like trying to grab water with your hand. Happiness is a serendipity—a product, a result. It is a state of mind, not a state of events. If you are not happy *NOW* what would make you happy *TOMORROW?* If you are not happy *WHERE* you are what place would produce happiness? Paul was happy in a jail; Caesar was miserable on a throne!

*HAPPINESS!*

(1) *HAPPINESS IS COURAGE!* The word courage has really fallen upon hard times! Being a dare-devil is not necessarily being courageous. Changing times have almost eliminated a coveting for courage. Yet, courage is a key to happiness. You cannot be happy while running away! You cannot be happy hiding behind a mask! Courage tackles problems and handles them.

(2) *HAPPINESS IS SERVICE!* Happy people are not trying to be happy—they are trying to be useful. John Mason Brown said, "I know no happy person who lives only for himself . . . true happiness comes from squandering ourselves for a purpose." "If you would be happy," Jesus said, "give yourself away."

(3) *HAPPINESS IS ANCHORAGE!* Read the Beatitudes of the Sermon on the Mount! Happy people were anchored in heart by the great principles of God! Days need to begin with God; they need to end with God! Happiness involves *CHARACTER!* It is not "what you have" but "who you are." Goodness precedes happiness! This is the simple key most have overlooked or denied in their quest for happiness.

ARE YOU HAPPY?

# "SISTER LANTER STRIKES AGAIN"

We all love Sister Lanter . . . so good, sweet, and wise. An encouragement to us all—yea the "spirit of the congregation" She has been an illustration in my preaching all over the brotherhood. Several years past this author bought a leisure suit—I don't think she liked it! When asked "How do you like this suit?" She replied, "I like the man in the suit." That's gentleness, tact, wisdom. Wouldn't the world be better if all practiced such kindness?

But—like the Pink Panther—she has "struck again." In the office the other day I gave her the usual "big hug" and the statement, "I love you." Her answer, "Do you know why you love me?" This caught me off guard. I countered, "No, why?" Her profound answer, "Because I first loved you." Simple, spiritual, sweet—yet so accurate.

She is so easily loved because she does love first! You never have to worry about her loving you. She may not like nor approve what you do—but you are "safe" with Sister Lanter! She loves you—will fight for you—will lovingly forgive you! You know she will never misuse nor mistreat you! So people turn to her, seek her out, love her! "Because she loves us first."

(1) This is a truth about God (1 John 4:10-11). We love God because He first loved us.

(2) This is a truth about life. We have the "cart before the horse." We demand that people love us before we love them. They do not, so we do not! But if we would only love others first—this provokes their response. We are not only supposed to love—but to love first! Sister Lanter does—and we all love her for it!

# "LESSONS FROM JOB"

Trouble comes . . . piles up . . . sometimes completely surrounds us! "When it rains it pours." Jesus was crucified; Paul was beheaded. None of us are exempt from pain, frustration, failure, and problems. But what does one do? This is the question! Quit? Give up? Blame God? Commit suicide? Become bitter? Run away? Conquer? Job lost ten children, all his possessions, his wife, his best friends, all in the space of a short time! *BUT JOB WON!* Turn to Job 1:20-22. How did Job win?

(1) *JOB WORSHIPPED GOD!* WHAT?!? In calamity Job worshipped! This is the crux of the matter! ". . . and worshipped." Job had the right concept about God. Life boils down to our concept of God. When God is big, problems are small. An inadequate or wrong concept of God displays itself in time of pressure!

(2) *JOB OBEYED!* WHAT?!? He did not wallow in self-pity; he did not blame nor withdraw. Read Job 1:20-22. He rent his robe, shaved his head, fell upon the ground! The right concept of God delivers obedience—even in troubling times.

(3) *JOB ACCEPTED!* WHAT?!? "Naked came I out of my mother's womb . . . God gives and takes away." Notice the order . . . 1-2-3! They must be in order. Man is prone to demand acceptance before obedience! Man demands—but Job worshipped and obeyed. When we worship and obey we find acceptance.

"Blessed be the name of the Lord."

# TIME, LIFE, AND YOU

Next to the Bible the best place to find sermon ideas is in the *Readers Digest!* I anticipate each issue. Good articles provoke decent thinking (Philippians 4). In a recent issue several points were made concerning the management of time. Paul said, "redeeming the time" (Ephesians 5:16). A time expert, Alan Lakein in his article made some observations:

(1) Most people do not think in terms of *minutes*. They waste all their minutes.

(2) The big question is, "What are your life time goals? If you don't have any—you ramble through life—not *living* life. Jesus had a one-track mind—the cross. Paul had one mind—Philippians 3:13, 14. Most people fail because they do not know what they want nor where they are going.

(3) How would you spend the next 5 years? *BE CARE-FUL!* Does this fit your *life time* goal? You may contradict yourself! Great power comes from well-defined goals.

(4) Do you make a daily list of the things you should do? Very simple, yet so productive. Every day is connected with all other days—your life. There is always enough time to do the important.

(5) Most people abuse or neglect the most productive hours of the day—8-11 A. M.

(6) Time is life.

# "CONTENTMENT"

*"Not that I speak in respect of want: for I have learned, in whatsoever state I am, therewith to be content . . . I can do all things through Christ which strengtheneth me."*
Philippians 4:11-14

Contentment? Not talked about much! Practiced even less! Are you contented? more contented? learning about contentment? It is the flower virtue—beautiful yet neglected. Several things are to be observed:

(1) Contentment must be *LEARNED!* Contentment is neither natural nor instinctive. It requires apprenticeship—development. But it can be learned! There is no excuse. Our great "I can do all things" is couched in this context!

(2) Paul has learned *HOW* to live! Living—contentment, are twins! Paul is not teaching passivity, stoicism, resignation. He is not seeking sympathy! He is teaching abundant living. Life transcends externals! He knows *HOW* to live.

(3) Contentment is not attained from human merit. Re-read verse 13. Re-read our point number 1! Contentment involves our relationship with Christ.

(4) Contentment is with difficulty in any circumstance. Sinful people poor do not become righteous people when rich—or educated—or powerful! Contentment may be more difficult with money, power, and success than adversity! Contentment is *WHO* you are—not *WHERE* you are or *WHAT* you have!

# "ON BEING 45"

30, 40, 45—these are the birthdays of evaluation? Who am I? What have I done? Where am I going? What happens next? At 45 you have experienced most of life's experiences —the thrill of victory and the agony of defeat.

Age can be humbling and depressing! When young dreams are the order of the day—grandiose, unrealistic, yet necessary and motivating. We are all going to be rich, powerful, and famous—the world remade in our image. At 45 dreams have become nightmares; it is obvious we will neither move nor shake the world! You can write all your accomplishments on the back of a postage stamp! The truth of life overwhelms! Man knows he is not "God"—most things are beyond his control!

Yet from this admission of realities and true self limits real life comes! Who said we were "God" to begin with? Who asked us alone to change the world? There are several things I now know at 45!

(1) *God is good!* I am a blessed man—Christian parents, a great family, a wonderful local church, faithful friends, physical health, numerous privileges and opportunities—I am a blessed man!

(2) *People are the name of the game.* In my mind I am neither young nor old! I am just "me." I do not wish to be a teen, 20, 30 yea even 40 again! 50, 60, 70 all sound exciting! Every age is better than the last! The little things, courtesies, investments in the lives of others are the real issues of life! To help anyone under his burdens brings eternal satisfaction. Life is worth living and the best things in life are still free!

P. S. Many have asked if I "quit preaching at 40"? I did— the brethren haven't discovered it yet!

# "ON DEATH AND DYING"

Elisabeth Kubler-Ross wrote a profound book about death—on *Death and Dying* which is now followed by *Death, The Final Stage of Growth.* She is a psychiatrist who has given her professional life to patients with terminal diseases and their families. Our culture denies, defies and ignores death! Death is a vital aspect of life. Actually, without death, life has lost much of its meaning. Dr. Kubler-Ross lists the stages patients and their families experience in the trauma of death!

(1) *DENIAL!* "No, not me." One cannot believe what he has been told. Various games, etc. are done, in effect, denying this premise. Some of the family never accept it. Many times, the patient hides to avoid family and friends.

(2) *ANGER!* "Why me?" I am young—things are just beginning good to me. Accepting death brings resentment—helplessness. God, society, family are all blamed. Remember —"God can take it."

(3) *BARGAINING!* "Yes, me, but." Give me until Christmas—or my birthday, until I finish this job. Good is given in exchange for time. Most of these promises, intentions are not kept.

(4) *DEPRESSION.* "Yes, me." The impact is now here. This is "preparatory grief." He does not want nor need the living anymore. So withdrawal, non-interest are in command.

(5) *ACCEPTANCE.* "Yes." No longer resignation but victory. It can be talked about, handled. The patient is ready.

*Death* will one day knock on your door.

# "JOY"

Joy is as rare as an honest man. The world is short now on so many things—land, energy, food—but the greatest shortage is joy. Nietzsche, the critic said, "I would believe in their salvation if they looked a little more like people who have been saved." *JOY!* Why is there not more joy?

(1) God is a creator of joy! 1 Timothy 6:15! God is a God—blessed, happy, joyous. Heaven is a joyous place. Joy reflects the purity and goodness of God. God is the source of joy.

(2) The Bible has one great promise—joy! The NT is a symphony of joy. Angels announced joy when Jesus was born; Jesus promised His disciples joy when He was under the shadow of the cross; He even said their joy would be full (John 15:10, 11); the book of Acts is triumphant joy forged in the crucible of persecution; the kingdom of God is joy; the fruit of the Spirit is joy.

(3) Joy is not just pleasure. Pleasure is a good stimulation of our senses which is short-lived and must be re-done. It can easily degenerate into indulgence and sin. Joy differs from "happines," which is best experienced through relationships with others.

(4) Joy is the fruit of the Spirit (Galatians 5:22-23). It is a fruit, not a work. It cannot be directly produced. It can be pruned by spiritual discipline, enriched through Bible study, strengthened by prayer, and matured in obedience! But it is a by-product, a serendipity, of a deep faith and a pure conscience!

# "THE END OF LIFE"

"Death is always new" . . . even in the intensive care unit death always strikes suddenly . . . death always shocks! Man has always defied and denied death. The new pope died within a few days. Airplane crashes kill hundreds. Teens are killed in various ways. There is a "human instinct" or "idea" about death.

(1) Man thinks many deaths are "premature." He was cheated! Just when he married, they had their first child, started making money, had things going his way! Man seemingly thinks there is a timetable to life—you are born, grow up, succeed, get extra old, then gently die! *IT AIN'T SO!* Man actually is bargaining with God! "Wait until we are ready, God, and we won't mind much." We dismiss many deaths: "Well, he was old and had lived his life."

(2) So death loses its sense of timing—at least to us! Death forgets its place . . . ended beginnings . . . interrupted middles. Is it conceit that makes us think that death should have a better sense of timing—or is it hope?

(3) "It is appointed unto man once to die." This gives priority to each day! There are no guarantees for tomorrow. Use what you have . . . milk each day of its duty and joy. Few lives, if any, are ever finished—they are simply, ended! All die prematurely! No one wants to live to be *100* unless he is *99!* The value of death lies within the context of life. Jesus gives *LIFE,* resurrection life. Learn about it!